Dilemmas of the Curriculum

Also in the Issues and Ideas in Education Series
edited by Robin Barrow, School of Education,
University of Leicester

Fantasy and Common Sense in Education
John Wilson

By the same author
Freedom and Authority in Education
L. H. Myers: A Critical Study
Education in an Industrial Society
Education and Values
Education, Culture and the Emotions
Culture, Industrialisation and Education
T. S. Eliot and Education
Studies in the History of Educational Theory
Vol. I: Artifice and Nature

Dilemmas of the Curriculum

G. H. BANTOCK

Emeritus Professor of Education
University of Leicester

A HALSTED PRESS BOOK

John Wiley & Sons
New York

First published in 1980 by Martin Robertson, Oxford.

Published in the U.S.A.
by Halsted Press, a division
of John Wiley & Sons, Inc.,
New York.

Library of Congress Cataloging in Publication Data

Bantock, Geoffrey Herman, 1914-
    Dilemmas of the curriculum.

"A Halsted Press book."
Bibliography: p.
Includes index.
    1. Education — Curricula. I. Title.
LB1570.B326   1980   375   80—11764
ISBN 0-470-26920-0

Typeset by Pioneer Associates, East Sussex.
Printed and bound in Great Britain by Richard Clay Ltd.,
The Chaucer Press, Bungay, Suffolk.

Contents

Acknowledgements

Some parts of this book have already appeared in print, in *Melbourne Studies in Education 1972* and in *Black Paper 1975*, though in most cases the borrowed material has been considerably re-cast. Nevertheless I am grateful to the editors and the publishers for permission to draw on some of the substance there incorporated. As ever, too, I am grateful to my wife for having discussed both the style and content with me and for having undertaken the task of preparing the index.

Introduction

I had already finished this book when I happened to take down from my shelves Lionel Trilling's *Beyond Culture*. There, in the first few pages, I read:

> The unargued assumption of most curriculums is that the real subject of all study is the modern world; that the justification of all study is its immediate and presumably practical relevance to modernity; that the true purpose of all study is to lead the young person to be at home in, and in control of, the modern world. [1966, p. 4]

This witness from an American university teacher of an implication that I had made into one of the central issues of the book I had just completed seemed too good to miss. For one thing, it provided an indication of the ubiquity of my theme; my impression that these things had gone at least as far, and indeed, under the influence of some of their major educational theorists, perhaps further, in the United States than in England was confirmed. For another, a strategic reference to the dilemma — as Trilling makes it appear in the outcome of his essay 'On the Teaching of Modern Literature' from which the extract is taken — might well alert the reader to the fact that the long historical analysis of the development of the curriculum he is just about to face and to which most modern writing on the curriculum will scarcely have accustomed him forms an integral part of the following argument and should not be regarded as a largely redundant prolegomenon to the meatier (because nearer contemporary) comments of the subsequent chapters. The social science orientation of present-day educational studies has so alerted us to the notion of change, and therefore to the necessity of being up to date, that the theorist who wishes to suggest that there may at least be some things that can be learnt from the past faces not so much a hostility as a disbelief manifest as a puzzlement. To focus on Trilling's statements and to suggest that they imply not an almost otiose account of contemporary practice but a dilemma provides a not inappropriate introduction to what follows.

CHAPTER 1

The Evolution of the Curriculum

I

The concept of a curriculum designates the aggregate of courses of study provided in an educational institution. There are two features of this definition that deserve attention — the notion of an aggregate and its reference to institutional life. Schools are concerned to transmit a digest of adult intellectual culture (in the evaluative sense of the word). A curriculum, therefore, implies that part of the adult culture thought important enough to be transmitted to the younger generation and within its grasp. As a complex, therefore, it is subject to psychological limitations; at the same time, the fact that it has become institutionalized implies at least a limited consensus within the society as to what is important for the continuity of the society's culture and way of life. Curricular changes, therefore, can be very revealing about the altered priorities assigned to various skills and intellectual disciplines and indicate, in some instances at least, profound reorientations in a society's existence. To become sufficiently central to the life of a society to warrant curriculum attention implies a degree of prior acknowledgement; for in their business of conservation the tendency is for educational institutions only to recognize the well established. (This, however, does not *necessarily* imply that such recognitions should always be endorsed.)

The notion of an aggregate also implies a certain coherence among the parts. This conception is confirmed by a consideration of the etymology of the word 'curriculum'. Initially it comes from the Latin, meaning 'a running', 'a race', and can be used to refer to the orbit of heavenly bodies. The notion of a set path, of something circumscribed and directed to a goal, seems to be built into its meaning. The idea of a race or a contest in running would seem to imply a coherence of effort among a number of elements brought into some sort of unity for the purpose in hand. Figuratively the word is used by Cicero to designate the 'course of our life' (*curriculum vitae*), and again the notion of integration, as well as a sense of direction, is implicit in the coherence of a life. It is not fanciful, then, to see in an academic curriculum not any chance collocation of skills and disciplines but something the parts of which cohere in certain terms. These terms are typically some principles — social, moral, intellectual, or a mixture of the three — binding together the various elements of the curriculum into some sort of unity of conception. In classical times, for instance, coherence seems to have been much more provided by the home; and the child was sent to a 'school' that was only intermittently institutionalized in the modern sense. Often 'school' existed in the open air at the meeting of ways (hence the origin of *trivium* and *quadrivium*,[1] the seven 'liberal' arts) or in odd rooms hired for specific purposes; children attended for various types of teaching given by people who often only met transiently, if at all, and who therefore had no proper institutional life and therefore collectively represented no overall aim or purpose. In this way what was taught lacked the coherence necessary to make it a curriculum in the normally accepted sense of the word — certainly the sense in which I am using it here. As Durkheim puts it, school (and the aggregate of courses which accompanies the setting up of a firm institutional life) 'could only emerge with the emergence of people in whose view the essence of human culture consists not in the acquisition of certain specific abilities or habits of mind but rather in a general orientation of the mind and the will' (1977, p. 30). Such schools only became institutionalized in the West during the middle ages; for medieval schools were tied to a Christian purpose, and Christianity involved a general disposition of mind and will, resulting from the act of conversion, which transformed the concept of education from one concerned with transmitting specific skills under haphazard conditions uninformed by any general orientation to one where the totality of the child's education was permeated by a very specific ethos and purpose. As Professor James Bowen puts it of medieval education:

Education . . . was a single process: it had an unquestioned
Christian ideology; an agreed curriculum in Latin based upon the
study of classical literature, both pagan and Christian; a single
pedagogy, that of the master instructing *ex cathedra;* and one
pervasive support system, involving progression from elementary
through grammar school, to university, all under the aegis of
Holy Church. [1975, p. xxi]

In general, in this book, I shall be dealing with what can be broadly
identified as the secondary curriculum, that for older children. Thus
I shall not concern myself with the petty or primary school.
Furthermore, I shall concentrate on what has, in the fullness of
time, become broadly identifiable as the 'common' curriculum for
secondary schools. I shall not therefore deal with developments
within forms of elementary education for senior pupils. These are of
great historical interest; but with the move towards comprehensive
education, the evolution of a 'common' curriculum which, in general,
follows historically 'secondary' patterns has raised the specifically
relevant dilemmas for the 1980s; and these dilemmas are not
confined to one country but exist in broad terms in all countries
where comprehensive schooling has been implemented.

II

Schooling thus became infused with a moral purpose which even
today is not altogether lost; at the same time the traditional linguistic
studies (the *trivium,* grammar, logic and rhetoric — the *quadrivium,*
the more 'scientific' subjects, arithmetic, geometry, astronomy and
music, was largely confined to higher forms of education), inherited
from classical times, as the name implies, became reoriented in
order to serve Christian ends. Thus grammar concerned itself with
the basic structure of the language and its categories — syntax and
various classifications to give it clarity and formal accuracy, a study
which, of course, demanded close attention to literary texts. Of the
two disciplines, rhetoric, which had formed so crucial an element in
the education of *doctus orator* of classical times because of its
political and legal usefulness, suffered a comparative eclipse during
the medieval period, when concern for ultimate 'truth' and its
contemplation tended to overshadow the more active commitment

of the orator, and logic (dialectic) assumed a correspondingly greater importance. Logic constituted, indeed, the science of understanding — and understanding rather than action was the aim of medieval education: its scope can be gleaned from the remarks by Hrabanus Maurus (c. 776-836). Through dialectic

> . . . we apprehend the origin and activity of the good, of Creator and creature; it teaches us to discover the truth and unmask falsehood; it teaches us to draw conclusions; it shows us what is valid in argument and what is not; it teaches us to recognize what is contrary to the nature of things; it teaches us to distinguish in controversy the true, the probable, and the wholly false. [quoted in Bowen, 1975, p. 19]

Such emphasis on logic (which, despite slight differences of significance, came to be used more or less interchangeably with dialectic) characterized the cathedral schools of the eleventh century; it becomes the main instrument of scholastic methodology in the twelfth and thirteenth centuries. Rhetoric, despite some attention paid to it by John of Salisbury in the twelfth century, only sprang to life as a school subject as a result of the humanist revolution of the fourteenth and fifteenth centuries. The humanist stress on action rather than contemplation, involvement in civic affairs rather than the reconciliation of philosophical views with the demands of faith and revelation, concern for morality rather than metaphysics, directed attention once more towards the art of persuasion based on the Ciceronian concept of *doctus orator*. The humanists fostered a refined stylistic content, purged on medieval Latin barbarities, and attention to the moral insights provided by classical and patristic literature. The framework, however, remained obstinately Christian, despite the growing humanist attention to political rather than to religious affairs; for most of the prominent humanists (including Erasmus, for instance) worked within the faith, even if many of them desired its purgation as currently established, and avoided the earlier, Augustinian emphasis on original sin.

Over a vast period of time, then, the basic curriculum of the *trivium* served a Christian purpose, albeit one which shifted its interest from other worldly to this worldly speculation. This indicates the coherence of purpose within certain mutabilities of emphasis which I have taken to characterize a curriculum. Nevertheless the revised orientation of the humanists contained within it implications which during the Renaissance were to destroy the medieval synthesis and gradually introduce a new principle of articulation: for the study of a past that included a divine revelation came to be substituted that of the world: 'experience'.

III

The bias of pre-seventeenth century education had been variously directed to both intellectual and behavioural objectives (corresponding in some degree to the passive and active aspects of classical Christian culture) but both scholastic and humanistic conceptions shared a common orientation to the past. That past was variously made up of Christian revelation, Aristotelian logical methodology and classical morality and eloquence (manifest latterly especially as 'style'). The basic aim of scholastic education had been to establish and preserve the sanctity of a prior revelation, that of humanist learning to deploy the values of classical literature in active politics. Fundamental concepts in terms of which one could interpret the medieval and Renaissance educational curriculum would have to include 'authority', 'imitation' and 'memory'. These concepts would refer both to the medium of scholastic and Renaissance education — principally Latin, with Greek and sometimes Hebrew added later — and to the subject-matter. (The 'authority' and consequent 'imitation' of classical stylistic models became much tighter with the coming of the humanists.) Thus the basic philosophical suppositions and axioms of medieval and Renaissance thinking were based on the authority of others: no thinker in these periods started, like Descartes, to build a philosophical system from the postulates of his own mental experience.

Yet the human mind has a tendency to wander a little even within guide-lines rigidly laid down for its operation; and Lane Poole, nearly a hundred years ago in his *Medieval Thought and Learning*, having indicated that in the middle ages 'we find nothing absolutely original', nevertheless conceded that there was 'never a time when the life of Christendom was so confined within the hard shell of its dogmatic system that there was no room left for individual liberty of opinion' (1932, pp. 1-3). This 'liberty' (which must not be confused with a modern lack of restraint) can perhaps best be clarified through an analysis of renaissance notions of 'imitation'.

IV

Undoubtedly Renaissance educational thinking about the curriculum contained within it the seeds of future transformations. 'Imitation', as understood by the best Renaissance minds, was to be distinguished from slavish copying. Certainly, Renaissance theorizing emphasized that man was 'fashioned, not born', hence the deployment of concepts like 'moulding' and 'forming' as operative in the upbringing of the young. Furthermore, an examination of humanist methodology in even the best schools brings out the stress on finding both material and style in former models; thus 'invention' (the discovering of the substance of discourse) initially implied recourse to the 'common places', traditional material derived from classical sources and latterly often contained in books of adages, 'useful sayings' (Erasmus produced an *Adagia,* a text-book of useful extracts) by which the pupil, writing his 'theme' in school, could induce an infusion of '*copia*' (or plentifulness of expression); only latterly did the notion come to assume something of modern implication of novelty. In addition, under humanist guidance, the study of actual stylistic devices — the order of sentences and the choice of language as well as the 'figures' of speech (of which, over a hundred were taught in Elizabethan England) — was detailed and severe. Thus Ascham's technique of double translation by which classical passages translated into English were re-translated into Latin by the pupil so that he could then compare his rendering with the original and hence learn to acquire the very language as well as the categories of thought characteristic of the classical experience gives a not unfair indication of the later severities of humanistic methodology (cf. Ascham, 1967).

The aim of this severity, paradoxically, was *not* to turn out 'apes of Cicero', slavish copyists of the master; the purpose was to encourage a high degree of internalization of the best writing so that the grasp acquired could then be redeployed in 'free' composition. The Renaissance grasped the essential truth that freedom of expression springs from mastery and is not a manifestation — except in a trivial, 'negative' sense — of untutored spontaneity. The aim of Renaissance education was to civilize the child and make him 'free' within the disciplines he had acquired, not simply to leave him to his own devices in the name of 'self-expression'.

Exact representation, then, was transcended in terms ultimately metaphysical. The educational aim was still delineated as seeking, in Aristotelian terms, to actualize a potential — but 'potential' was a necessarily ill-defined concept that was limited only by human conceptions of the ideal. Renaissance education, whatever short-comings it may have had, was permeated by notions of excellence.

V

We seem to be departing far from any curriculum consideration. Not so. For the bald areas of concern — grammar, logic, rhetoric — are so alien to modern views that they require some clarification if their significance in educational terms is to take on any meaning. Furthermore, my exposition has induced me to introduce two notions which, further elucidated, will enable me to indicate curricular potentialities highly relevant to future developments. It will not have escaped the reader's notice that both medieval and Renaissance education were essentially verbal — words (and incidentally spoken words) were the inescapable tools of logical and rhetorical training, both of which, as I have indicated, were preceded by the rigours of grammar, the basis of linguistic grasp. Durkheim's brilliant analysis of the significance, for later developments in logic, of grammatical classifications can be recommended to the reader (grammar, he argues, is no longer in the Carolingian era 'a purely verbal study; it is an early form of the study of logic' — 1977, p. 59); I prefer, in view of my commitment to later developments, to concentrate on humanist rhetoric and its implications. Clearly words have referents; and the relationships of words to 'things' occupied educationists (and others, for that matter) for many centuries. Erasmus was clear in his educational priorities: 'All knowledge falls into two divisions: the knowledge of things [*rerum*] and the knowledge of words [*verborum*]; and words come first [*verborum prior*]' (cf. Woodward, 1964, p. 162). It is true he assigns a greater value to 'things'; but he goes on to point out that knowledge of 'things' (by which he meant 'truths' about human affairs, facts or empirical knowledge) is dependent on linguistic awareness: 'For ideas are only intelligible to us by means of the words that describe them.' So training in language constituted the essential propaedeutic to any understanding of the world and had educational priority. To put it another way, in the Erasmian scheme 'instruction precedes experience'; one must approach the world with a mind prepared to deploy the relevant concepts: 'A long and manifold experience is, beyond doubt, of great profit, but only to such as by the wisdom of learning have acquired an intelligent and informed judgment.' For 'philosophy teaches us more in one year than our own individual experience can teach us in thirty' (p. 191).

Readers knowledgeable in the ways of current educational theorizing will doubtless appreciate my references and the ignorant will pick up their significance later. To indicate the essentially bookish and linguistic approach of Erasmus, his remark 'What can men learn from trees?' (a purely rhetorical question!) and his assertion that within the literatures of Greece and Rome 'are contained all the knowledge which we recognise as of vital importance to mankind' (p. 163) should suffice. Yet we are on the verge of the beginnings of a profound transformation of curriculum orientation. With benefit of hindsight, one might detect some clues to this in Erasmus' frequent appeal to 'nature'. Partly this constitutes an appeal to the metaphysically pre-ordained conception of right development just noted — what he terms an 'innate capacity for being trained' and a 'native bent towards excellence' (p. 191; the concept of nature is used normatively). But sometimes it has empirical implications, resulting from observation: hence his appeal to children's 'instinct of imitation and a delight in activity', which 'nature has planted' in them (p. 198). Typically humanists — and they are not alone in this — tend to confuse the normative and the empirical usages of the concept. But together with their appreciation of individual natures as offering differing capacities, their observation of child behaviour reveals an incipient empirical element in their theorizing: philosophically it aligns them with nominalists (those who defined reality in terms of particulars) rather than realists (those who conceived the real in terms of the 'universal'). After all, Erasmus' methodological emphasis was on *practice,* not rote learning.

VI

It was a friend and younger contemporary of Erasmus, Juan Luis Vives, who signalled a further significant breach in pure humanist bookish orthodoxy. There had been much in the Renaissance to encourage a realization of the importance of observation and direct experience of the external world through visualisation: technical developments (we know that even medieval technology was more advanced than once thought), perspective in painting, the planned city rather than the haphazardness of medieval 'growth' — all pointers to a fundamental reorientation of knowledge from one that arose out of verbal intercourse between people to one based on the visual apprehension of the external world (cf. Ong, 1962, pp. 69-70).

Vives makes his initial contribution to this reorientation. He insists that knowledge is expanding, not fixed, that the ancients had not known it all:

> It is clear, if we only apply our minds sufficiently, we can judge better over the whole round of life and nature than could Aristotle, Plato or any of the ancients . . . Truth stands open to all. It is not yet taken possession of. Much of truth has been left for future generations to discover. [Watson, 1913, pp. 8-9]

'Truth stands open to all' — there could have been no statement more redolent of the future: no longer encapsulated in ancient authority but 'democratized' and resulting from the direct contact of mind and world. Language no longer fulfils ornamental or expressive functions; its 'educational value . . . is in proportion to its apt suitability for supplying names to things' (Watson, 1913, p. 92).

One must not overdo Vives' commitment to the empirical; he ranks still as a humanist and in no way deprecates books (though he *is* cool on poetry, which constitutes not 'real life but a kind of painting' and is for leisure, as a spice rather than nourishment); but the orientation of the 'real' is undergoing a further shift in the direction of the particular — and this is, of course, to have profound curricular implications.

And then, a further straw in the wind, there was the scepticism of Montaigne's 'Que sais-je?' (What do I know?). Starting from the constantly shifting perspectives of his own mind, Montaigne was led to doubt — intermittently at least, for it is characteristic of his chameleon-like nature to be consistently inconsistent — the current manifestations of contemporary culture. Man's reason was a more unstable thing than he realized; standpoints were relative, not absolute; eloquence should give way to a mode of communication that was 'natural and simple' (*naif*). These are early hints of a cult of the less sophisticated: 'I wish I could limit myself to the language of the Paris markets' (1958, p. 80). In Montaigne we have the spectacle of a man deploying very many of the traditional devices of rhetoric (including his very self-presentation as a '*naif* '!) to undermine the whole traditional linguistic and rhetorical structure.

VII

The humanists had, however, accomplished much. Their most significant achievement had been the civilizing of the lay aristocracy: they had made literacy and cultivation essential concomitants of social and political responsibility — in terms, indeed, that have persisted in considerable measure almost down to our own time. Though cultural changes of the profoundest importance and significance are now historically imminent, it must not be forgotten that humanist interests persisted among certain socially powerful sections of the school population as the predominating curricular factor for a very long time in both England and America. Furthermore, the 'humanities' as that term is understood today, expressed latterly in the vernacular rather than in the classical languages, persist as factors in a much extended curriculum through their commitment to, in some sense of the term, the study of man.

The other great and significant contribution of the humanists had been their stress on *knowledge* — knowledge, of course, of a special kind, that to be found largely within the pages of authoritative texts, but knowledge (in medieval times mostly the prerogative of 'clerks') nevertheless, with its necessary affiliations with mind. They initiated, indeed, an extension of consciousness which constitutes the most significant achievement of the West. To Rabelais, the classics were sources of information leading to an encyclopaedic learning much more than sources of stylistic purity; elements of this Renaissance encyclopaedism — its concern for *uomo universale* and the 'circle of knowledge' — feed into seventeenth-century pansophic ideals and initiate our twentieth-century acceptance that all knowledge constitutes a good. Montaigne could never have queried what he knew if, as an aristocrat, he had nevertheless not been asked to *know* something. Philosophically the humanists prepared the way for the shift from medieval preoccupations with ontology to seventeenth-century concerns with epistemology. Bacon's *Advancement of Learning* and Descartes' 'cogito ergo sum' (I think, therefore I am) both owe a great deal to humanist preoccupation with learning as an essential element in the right ordering of social life.

So, 'knowledge is power' the humanists might have proclaimed: in their case persuasive power, the power of argument which combined content with eloquence — in a word 'style', a concept with implications for a whole way of life; and it must not be forgotten that, ultimately, their aim was moral and their attention concerned with manners as well as ethics. The study of letters that formed the core of their curriculum had implications for conduct. 'Knowledge' implied knowing *how* to behave as well as knowing *what* to say; and thus power was exercised (as courtiers for instance) as much in the elegance of their behaviour, their 'politeness', as in their effortless deployment of convincing and significant argument and persuasion. This aspect of 'curriculum' during the humanist period must not be forgotten: for it explains curricular accretions in the life of the courtier such as dancing and the arts, aspects of an extended conception of rhetoric (was not gesture an essential element in declamation?).

Yet the phrase is, in fact, Bacon's; and the knowledge he referred to was significantly different. It was, to begin with, based on experience of the external world, of 'things'. The advanced educational thinkers of the seventeenth century perpetually reiterated the need for attention to 'things not words', and the focal point of 'things' was matter in motion. Furthermore, it was associated specifically with mind, 'understanding'; its orientation was cognitive — it did not encompass the whole person for, in essence, it was indifferent to manners, though not, initially at least, to morals. Indeed, in its implementation it addressed an appeal to very different sections of the community from that on which humanism had made its impact. Humanism was essentially aristocratic in the sense that its appeal was to an elite. Certainly it was an aristocracy in which there was beginning to be a limited degree of mobility — a mobility assisted in part by the educational qualification that humanism as an ideal provided. For humanism was, in some degree, a means to social advancement; but it implied an esoteric and restricted world of alien tongues (alien, that is, from the vernacular) and a refined literary appreciation. It became — and remained — the educational curriculum of the ruling class.

Bacon's 'knowledge', however, assumed a common world, one open to the inspection of all; furthermore, it consciously drew on the 'experience' of artisans and countrymen as a possible — indeed, necessary — source for its definition. Logic, rhetoric, the elegancies of an alien literature, were scornfully cast aside (though as Latin continued to constitute the language even of scientific scholarship for a time, it remained a necessary tool). The aim, according to Bishop Sprat in his *History of the Royal Society* (1667) was to 'reject all the amplifications, digressions and swellings of style' — in a word 'the colours of Rhetorick' — in favour of a 'mathematical plainness of speech, preferring the language of Artizans, Country-men, and Merchants, before that, of Wits, or Scholars' (quoted in Willey, 1934, p. 212). The new knowledge was a 'democratic' knowledge, derived from a common experience and it sought a plainer utterance. Furthermore, it lacked, in its commitment to empirical fact, a moral value dimension implicit in the old 'literary' knowledge. Morality remained explicit in the undertaking, but it included no specific content.

'Experience', indeed, came to be a key concept: the word used in earlier expositions was often 'sensation', for the experience intended was that revealed by direct contact of the senses with the external world. The precise nature of that relationship has become a major philosophical issue from the seventeenth century down to our own times. Was there a world 'out there' or was the world ultimately the creation of mind? In either case it was mind functioning cognitively on which attention was focused. The humanists had appealed to 'reason' — but it was a reason that worked in terms of literary judgement and the proper arrangement of traditional materials; now it was to be a reason that operated to discover the regularities of the external world and to acquire the means by which those regularities could be exploited for technical purposes — 'experiments of light' and 'experiments of fruit', as Bacon called them. Nature, to be conquered, must be obeyed: the Baconian paradox reveals at once the submission of mind to natural events and, at the same time, the ability of mind to subsume such happenings under general headings by the application of mathematical principles. Such knowledge as to how nature worked could then be translated into forms of power, by which nature could be 'vexed' and to some degree tamed.

So was initiated a movement for curriculum reform that would take cognizance of the new sources of understanding and control. At first it coexisted with the fundamental religious and Christian orientation of previous ages: it's difficult to decide just how religiously inclined Bacon himself was, but he certainly went through the motions of assigning unto faith that which was faith's — sufficiently, indeed, to captivate the puritans, who adopted the power and control he offered them as essential elements in their millenarian aspirations. The new empiricism offered opportunities of progress. But more, it assumed the character of a religious operation in so far as it laid bare the wonders of God's handiwork. It cannot be too strongly insisted that the move towards curricular reform through the inclusion of what can be broadly termed, 'scientific' subjects was initially justified on religious, millenarian and eschatalogical grounds: 'knowledge' bore witness to puritan applications and efforts in their own salvation. Much of this is clear in Comenius who equates human 'art', 'nature' and divine revelation as facets of the same 'truth' about men and the world: the three revealed a harmonious purposive striving fulfilling the divine law. But, of course, a developing scientific orientation had to shed any teleological implications.

VIII

Yet, initially, the new 'knowledge', like the old, existed within a Christian framework. While this persisted, of course, mind could not achieve cognitive autonomy: its workings, like that of nature, were teleologically oriented. But, under the impact of a thorough-going empiricism, the workings of 'nature' gradually came to be viewed as neutral operations obeying their own internal dynamics:

God became the First Mover only of what, in other respects, operated like a machine. The demythologization of nature was (largely) accomplished during the Enlightenment — I say 'largely' because, in so far as man was part of nature, his commitment to a world of values ensured the perpetuation, at least, of teleological overtones in many future references to the natural world.

In the process, mind achieved a degree of autonomy: psychologically it operated according to certain putatively discernible laws; epistemologically it was directed towards what manifested an equivocally 'objective' 'truth'. It was from mind that one might infer the nature and human limits of the world, not from revelation: Locke's study of the Understanding (partly a job of demolition: he conceived of himself as an 'under-labourer in clearing the ground a little, and removing some of the rubbish that lies in the way to knowledge' — 1947, p. xxiii) was intended to 'see what *objects* our understandings were, or were not, fitted to deal with' (p. xx). Those objects, it will be inferred, included the objects of the material world ('things') and 'reflections' on them and their workings. If the humanists had been empirically blinkered ('what can men learn from trees'), the empirics were metaphysically obtuse. Locke, by banishing any conception of innate ideas, became, like Descartes and Bacon before him, an implicit advocate of the Fresh Start. Reasoning from first principles came to replace Memory as the source of recommended educational endeavour. Comenius who, heaven knows, was an extraordinary amalgam of traditional metaphysical and contemporary empirical elements, was bald in his assertion 'men must . . . be taught to become wise by studying the heavens, the earth, oaks, and beeches, *but not by studying books'* (1896, p. 302; my italics). The contrast with Erasmus could hardly be more extreme.

So now have evolved two great principles of curricular coherence: Memory and Observation, historical culture and immediate sense impression, the metaphysical and the empirical, Words and Things. At first sight it looks positively cosy: humanism deals with the study of man, the empirics provide the wherewithal for the study of the world apart from man — extend the curriculum to take cognizance of the new discoveries and all will be well.

IX

Naturally, it was not as simple as that. For one thing the schools, apart from a few dissenting academies, were not prepared either ideologically or practically to include the new subjects in their curriculum. 'Scientific' subjects suffered from inferior status and until late in the nineteenth century, appeared to any extent only in the somewhat eccentric foundations of 'progressive' educators, or in dissenting academies. But this did not mean that at the level of thought the new scientific interests did not have important repercussions that were profoundly to affect curricular provision in the future. Modern curricular dilemmas cannot be understood without some reference to the ideological conflicts that arose as a result of the impact of scientific ideas on the traditional culture.

If in earlier times metaphysics (in which, of course, I would include theology) hindered empirical investigations, we have just seen (in Locke) that the empirics desired release from metaphysics; hence a growing hostility to religion, and indeed to anything that could be thought a 'fiction' — poetry for example. Even Renaissance theorists had been in some degree worried about the fictional element in verse, though they had made letters the focal point of their curriculum. Now, in Bacon's phrase, it 'was time to come out of the theatre'. 'There is no gold to be mined in Parnassus', urged Locke (1922, p. 141); if your child should happen to have a poetic vein, his general advice was to knock it out of him.

Underlying the dispute there were, of course, conflicting views of the 'nature' of man. From being part natural, part supernatural, the question arose as to whether he was not better regarded as a purely natural phenomenon. If 'things' could be categorized and mastered, would not man's secrets yield to an analogous scientific observation? After all, he had always been accepted as, in part, a natural phenomenon; clear away the metaphysical debris and he would stand unveiled as equally subject to scientific 'law' as any other natural phenomenon. The leap was there to be made and — a little uneasily — some of those who belonged to the eighteenth-century Enlightenment made it.

But there were difficulties about the step. Man in his development was indubitably a product equally of culture and of nature: indeed, 'nature' itself, as has already been made clear, was a highly ambiguous concept with frequent normative overtones. To introduce the necessity of nature into the world of man was in effect to risk confusing fact with value: though there *were* 'natural' limits to man's achievement both physical and mental (e.g. he could not fly unaided, some were 'stupid' others 'clever'), there were also opportunities for choice — for, demonstrably, what was characterized as 'natural' by one person (i.e. in accordance with man's nature) was not so characterized by another. Thus to dismiss men's 'fictions' as unreal was to ignore the fact that man had claims to be regarded as a fiction-creating being, the means through which he expressed his 'ideals'. Values were not *facts* of mental life in the sense that desires were — and could not be categorized in the same way. The very phrase 'the natural man' could be revealed as a persuasive ploy to urge one implicit set of values rather than another by cashing in on the favourable reactions reference to 'nature' fostered.

Any attempt, then, to reduce man's mental functioning to inexorable psychological law was doomed to failure, though the attempt has important educational repercussions. Indeed, it stimulated two very different approaches which are still, in some degree, with us. On the one hand, it offered the possibility of man's complete formation (with strong egalitarian implications) as a result of building up the 'right' associations through presenting them correctly; on the other hand, it fostered an extreme form of individual autonomy — it made interference problematic if not downright dangerous.

In the former case it was assumed that human nature was very much the same everywhere — and that differences arose from different environmental stimuli, different formative influences, different *education.* Locke *sometimes* seems to be taking this line: 'of all the men we meet with, nine parts of ten are what they are, good or evil, useful or not, by their education' (1922, p. 25). Hartley and the utilitarians were capable of sustaining much the same position; hence James Mill assumes that his readers will readily grant that 'all the difference which exists between classes or bodies of men is the effect of education' (1931, p. 12). It was a question of building up the correct associations, of producing 'certain sequences [of ideas], rather than others' (p. 17). Hartley believed that if this was done, men would become equal. This is to enthrone the educator with a vengeance — for it was his job to build up the associations; curriculum flourishes triumphantly. Furthermore, it was to conceive man largely in terms of his mind, the seed ground for 'associations'.

The latter view depended on the notion of endogenous development, of 'unfolding' from within. Its favourite metaphoric comparison is between child and plant. It appears recognizably but fleetingly in Comenius; it is implicit in some of Rousseau's appeals to 'follow nature' and certainly in his view of 'negative' education. It manifests itself briefly but overtly with all the inflexibility of law in Pestalozzi: 'Life develops human powers, even under the most diverse circumstances, in accordance with unchanging laws which apply equally whether the child concerned crawls in the gutter or is heir to the throne' (1910, p. 291).

Taken literally, this would mean that men operated according to necessity in the same way that the mechanical universe of the time followed its preordained path. However, Pestalozzi modified his blunt espousal of a human 'law'. Having said that 'growth of the tree is like that of man' he admits to the presence of a 'higher spirit' in man which is 'free to allow his sensory nature and sensory environment to bring about his ruin, or to work against and overcome them' (pp. 190-1). But law still operates strongly within his system: education must work in 'harmony with the laws which develop human powers'; and the teacher is likened to a gardener whose role is 'only' to watch 'lest any external force should injure or disturb' (p. 195). Froebel took much the same position.

Now, despite the fact that none of these theorists consistently followed their implied policy of non-interference, curriculum can be seen to be offered a subordinate place. Though they do not constitute the main line of educational development, they contribute to the evolution of an alternative tradition in progressivism. I shall have more to say about progressivism's view of the curriculum in due course; but it should already be clear that subject matter is in some degree in danger of disintegration and that psychological factors clearly predominate over the internal logic of the disciplines. Certainly progressivism has initiated a changed conception of the functioning of mind: it is no longer conceived of as a spatial entity, a repository — implying what Freire has termed the 'banking' theory of knowledge, in which knowledge is deposited *in* the mind; instead it has been conceived as a tool, an instrument — in its extreme form, an instigator of revolutionary praxis, 'that is, with *reflection* and *action* directed at the structures to be transformed' (Freire, 1972, p. 96).

X

What, however, for the moment I wish to pick up as what developed as the main line of educational thinking is the stress already noted on the centrality of *mind* in the designation of what is to be taught. (It will, of course, be understood that classical humanism continued to be defended nearly down to our own times.) The purpose behind the development of mind might be an instrumental one (e.g. to promote happiness or some sort of moral or social good) or it might be conceived of as an end in itself; but in either case the formation plays a central role. I have urged that experience ('sensation', 'observation') is to become a new determining factor in the delineation of curriculum. But 'experience' is Janus-faced: in one direction it looks towards mind, in the other towards world; there can be no 'experience' without an experiencing subject. From medieval times at least, consciousness has formed part of the etymology of the word. So the views taken of mind, both psychological in its mode of behaviour and philosophical in the determination of its proper objects of knowledge, come to be crucial factors in thinking about what is to be taught. Knowledge is constituted of those aspects of reality graspable by mind — this was the positive aspect of Locke's work of demolition. What could be accepted as knowledge now sought to revise the old classical curriculum, subject only to the psychological restrictions that the new awareness of childhood imposed. Consciousness underwent a further expansion.

But, of course, if mind determines what is taught, what is taught also determines mind. In their haste to demolish metaphysics and superstition, some of the eighteenth-century philosophers had tended to forget this. They had prised mind free from its traditional supports and had sent it out on its voyage of discovery 'with nothing more than the senses and the reason [it stood] up in', as Mr Antony Quinton puts it (1971, p. 201). Here we have the origin of that concept of mental 'autonomy' that so exercises educational philosophers in our own day. They have built up, indeed, a set of concepts very different from those that prevailed among the humanists. They are concepts that cluster round the notion of 'autonomy': appeals to 'reason' and 'evidence', objections to 'indoctrination', approved words like 'freedom' and 'equality'. These are matched by an acceptance of the importance of the 'forms of knowledge' (for their view of freedom is positive rather than negative). In all this they are truly the heirs of the Enlightenment.

And so we begin to evolve a conception of a revised curriculum that arises out of the interplay of mind and world; and the world that has educational priority among some of the more advanced thinkers, who are impressed by the extensions of knowledge that have taken place as a result of scientific observation, is that revealed to the *senses.* Here is where Rousseau, following Locke in this respect, began the education of his Emile, in the world that he could observe in some way:

> He wants to touch and handle everything; do not check these movements which teach him invaluable lessons. Thus he learns to perceive the heat, cold, hardness, softness, weight or lightness of bodies, to judge their size and shape and all their physical properties, by looking, feeling, listening, and, above all, by comparing sight and touch. [1943, p. 31]

Here is the origin of the 'object' lesson.

But, of course, even the practical educator discovers quite quickly that such a process is subtler than at first sight it seems; and indeed, Rousseau by mentioning notions like 'judging' and 'comparing' immediately implies that simple observation is not enough. Out of the buzz and disorder of pure sense impressions some order must be introduced: *how* does the mind judge and on *what* does it exercise itself. Rousseau very quickly has Emile conflating certain selected phenomena in a highly sophisticated way — witness the story of the conjuror and the duck that, influenced by a magnet, swings in one direction at the apparent command of the mountebank: 'The study of physics is begun' (1943, p. 138). Now to pick out of the totality of the scene the element of *regularity* implies an awareness that certain behaviour is significant and certain is not.

And so inevitably the mechanisms of significance come into question and one is led to inquire into the means by which mind is led to structure experience as well as about the 'meaning' of what is so structured: one is inevitably concerned with both the psychological enabling powers of mind and the logical interrelationships presented by world. That the precise relationship between the two is a matter of the greatest philosophical subtlety does not worry the practical educationist too much: he simply assumes — rightly for his purposes — that there is mind and there is subject-matter and he asks how the 'one' acquires the other and how, at the same time, the 'other' can assist in the training of the one.

XI

And so there came to be a proliferation of psychological theories as to how mind went about its business — indeed, a variety of views about the philosophical nature of mind itself. Inevitably this, in due course, had consequences for the implementation of curriculum. Perhaps the most influential theory, which in its modern form probably dates from Wolff's *Rational Psychology* that appeared in 1734, considered that the mind was made up of a number of separate faculties, a view, indeed, that persisted into the earlier years of the twentieth century. As to how these 'faculties' were to be 'trained' — what subject-matter would best assist their evolution — there came to be two broad views. One was that there were certain very high level 'subjects' which possessed excellent potential for general training, a training that led to the overall disciplining of the mind and made its various faculties highly susceptible to employment in other fields. Several subjects attracted this sort of attention — and not surprisingly, in view of the vested interests involved, the study of the classical languages was held to be peculiarly suited to this type of mind exercise. This involved the doctrine known as the transfer of training: the discipline acquired could be transferred to other purposes. Mathematics, which had already gained a certain place on the traditional curriculum, was also regarded as eminently suited to this type of discipline.

By this means, conservative supporters of the long-established and persisting humanist classical disciplines fought a strong rearguard action: initially, at least, it was not necessary to transform the traditional curriculum.

I have no hesitation in saying [proclaimed the Head of a Cambridge

College] that, on the average, boys trained on the classical side of our public schools make better men of science, of medicine, of law, than the boys who come to the University from the modern side; for the classics develop the power of sustained and orderly thinking. [quoted by Adams, 1912, p. 211]

Now it had long been the humanist case that anyone who entered on the great professions of law or medicine would benefit by having been initiated into the *trivium* beforehand; but the argument was sustained on general cultural grounds (a lawyer would be the better for being a gentleman) rather than on strictly psychological ones. The implication now was that the classical training would have a direct bearing on the mental processes necessary for the pursuit of the law, or scientific studies, or whatever.

Unfortunately, it largely was not true; and research helped to destroy the case for any general transfer: transfer only took place when the mental processes involved in the two disciplines were analagous. So an alternative form of the disciplinary argument lay in width of contact. It becomes a matter of moment that the different disciplinary powers attributed to a wide variety of subjects (mathematics for accuracy, history for judgement, science for observation, etc.) should all be represented in a broad curriculum. Here, breadth rather than concentration upon a few with peculiarly wide powers of mental training (so considered) now becomes the desired aim. Here is assisted the extension of the curriculum: the 'circle of knowledge' (a term that looks back in some degree to the encyclopaedism of the later Renaissance) must encompass the 'circle' of faculties; science could find its way in under this aegis.

XII

There are, however, other grounds on which extension and consequent breadth can be recommended. This arose out of the disciplinary power attributed not to the different subject areas but to their *content*. It gradually became generally recognized that the best way to communicate skill in any particular direction is to give practice in that direction. The person whose psychological system derived directly from the 'circle' of thought was Herbart. This is not the place for an exhaustive account of the Herbartian theory except to indicate that it is one that places a great emphasis on the role of knowledge: through it, in the form of what he terms 'apperception mass', the whole mental being of the pupil evolves. Herbart, indeed, believed in neither innate ideas nor innate faculties: knowledge constituted an organon, an instrument that was constitutive of all functioning of the 'soul' (mind). The child starts with a blank page of mind, without even the original synthesizing power attributed to it by Kant: as ideas are received they cohere into 'masses' which gradually come to fill the forefront of consciousness and further ideas are assimilated by such ideas already built up. The original equipment of the 'soul' merely enables self-preservation: it becomes 'enriched with a content, not through the development of any germ-like faculties, but solely through the growth of the ideas that experience creates within us' (de Garmo, 1895, p. 31). Such experience in any ordered way is specifically in the hands of the teacher, whose job it is so to order it that it becomes assimilable to the 'masses' already there, which the child initially brings with him to school.

Here, then, we have a theory in which mind is almost entirely the creation of 'experience' and which elevates content and the teacher (as the one who makes content graspable) as of prime importance. Here, indeed, is a psychology that is almost exclusively curriculum oriented. Herbart neglects 'the constitutive equipment of the mind, [and] fixes his attention solely on the production, reproduction, fusion, arrest, and general interaction of ideas' (de Garmo, 1895, p. 32); and these ideas come initially from without. New ideas are acquired on the basis of what has already been built up: curriculum must therefore be so managed that it reinforces and extends what is already there — this is where the skill of the teacher comes in; but, however arranged to become palatable, curriculum rules.

It is through the nature of the teacher's presentation that interest is aroused. Indeed, the aim of Herbartian education was constituted by the eliciting of a 'many-sided' interest through which the child actually desires to assimilate knowledge and experience in its various manifestations. In this context, the word I wish to emphasize is 'many-sided'. As the mind is, in the last resort, only what has been presented to it, and the morality that was the ultimate end of his educational system sprang not from an independent faculty of will but had its roots in thought — 'the combinations and total effect of the acquired ideas' (Selleck, 1968, p. 232) — it behoved the educator to spread his net widely. Concepts like 'many-sided' and the 'circle of thought' imply extension as well as internal coherence. Herbartians stress the need for concentration and correlation so that masses of ideas may cohere; but they also urge the necessity for range. In any case, 'interest' was intended to refer not to teaching devices adopted to make learning palatable, but to the result of learning — the fostering of a mental excitement to look abroad. And so Herbart, despite a certain liking for humanistic studies, insisted on a wide curriculum and considered that *realia* 'are at least as much a legitimate part of a complete education' as humanistic ones (quoted by Selleck, 1968, p. 235).

Herbartianism made no serious impact on English education until the 1890s — when it very quickly had a considerable effect on teacher training and educational thought at secondary level. Such influence was hardly surprising, for the ground had already been well prepared by others. There had, as already indicated, been encyclopaedists since earlier times. But, as scientific developments themselves reinforced educational theorizing, insistent demands for a more inclusive curriculum grew. Matthew Arnold had based his own curricular recommendations on the idea of the 'circle of knowledge': he believed that those who inclined to the study of nature should have some notion of the humanities, and those who inclined to the humanities should have some notion of the phenomena and laws of nature. His views had been echoed by Newman: the Cardinal, in his pursuit of the 'expansion of mind', demonstrated great friendliness to science. Thomas Huxley had pronounced his view that 'for the purpose of attaining real culture, an exclusively scientific education is at least as effectual as an exclusively literary education' (1902, p. 141). Herbert Spencer's advocacy is well known. 'Popular' attacks on the traditional exclusive attention to humanistic studies again much pre-dated the general reform of the curriculum. The *Edinburgh Review,* for instance, had urged the widening of the curriculum to include modern subjects in 1809 and again in 1830.

These various influences exercised a decisive effect on the famous Regulations for Secondary Schools of 1904, helping to confirm the view of faculty education that stressed width of training rather than the notion of mental discipline derived from a few subjects. Science had already entered the English higher grade schools and organized science schools increasingly during the eighties and nineties — to an extent, indeed, that drew an unfavourable legal judgment which made such work in elementary schools against the law and had the long-term effect of diverting science to the curricula of secondary schools (Gordon and Lawton, 1978, p. 123). Suitably liberalized, it found a place in these essentially elitist Regulations, which owed a great deal to Morant's determination — he was influenced by faculty considerations — to provide at once width and yet an essentially liberal education, unsullied by practicalities. Instruction, it is urged,

> must be such as gives a reasonable degree of exercise and development to the whole of the faculties, and does not confine this development to a particular channel, whether that of pure and applied science, of literary and linguistic study, or of that kind of acquirement which is directed simply at fitting a boy or girl to enter business in a subordinate capacity with some previous knowledge of what he or she will be set to do. [quoted by Clarke *et al.*, n.d., p. 40]

This concern for width and academic purity has persisted in England, relatively untouched, until nearly today despite attacks in the name of relevance. Though the arguments in its favour no longer depend on faculty psychology, the insistence on the centrality of knowledge and mind persists, the intention being that the rewards of learning should be at least initially intrinsic. Prestige, for instance, has rested still with pure rather than applied science.

The final confirmation of a scientific component in the curriculum — with the social sciences (economics, sociology) seeking entrance at sixth form level by the mid-1960s — marks a cultural reorientation of the profoundest significance, at least for our elite education. Classical humanism finally suffered defeat and a new type of knowledge, one directed to empirical actuality, gradually assumed a cultural predominance: thus it has gradually imported its quantitive methods into traditionally humanistic subjects like history and geography; even literature is regarded as revelatory of process rather than as a depository of didactic, moral wisdom.

My account has concentrated on the English scene: yet, globally, the period 1870-1900 can be identified as the one within which in a number of western countries, and especially America, the teaching of science became confirmed as a major innovation. In the United States, for instance, the Academies, largely private institutions, had previously challenged the predominance of the (Latin) grammar schools with a more practical curriculum which had often included scientific and technical subjects; but the education given still preserved classical studies and Latin remained one of the three most studied subjects in the curriculum (Sizer, 1964, p. 36); bookish studies predominated. As the Academy, a rural rather than an urban institution (pp. 40-1), gave way to the public high school of the urban areas, the sciences entered more fully into the curriculum. Thus in 1893 the Committee of Ten report resolved the debate over classical and scientific studies by making such studies equivalent in the major job of improving intellectual qualities by disciplining the mind: 'for this purpose, all of the principle subjects might do' (Dropkin *et al.,* 1965, p. 153). Within a decade most American schools had accepted these proposals, and despite further changes in the ethos of the high school following the promulgation of the Cardinal Principles — which initiated the comprehensive high school long before it appeared in any of the European countries — scientific and technical elements in the curriculum retained a place in the elective curriculum. Indeed, the very concept of a comprehensive high school would have been impossible without the culturally homogenizing implications of a scientific uniformitarianism derived from the eighteenth-century Enlightenment, which affected rootless America initially more deeply than the more historically structured European societies; they, however, are following suit.

XIII

There has, inevitably, crept into the discussion one concept that requires further elucidation, for it has undoubtedly exercised a perennial influence on the discussion of curricular objectives, as it persists in doing today — that of a 'liberal education'. From Plato to Robert Hutchins and Professor Hirst the notion has played an important part in determining the curriculum: its chief influence has been to inhibit appeals to *immediate* practicality — and it has often prevented, for instance, the development of a more specialized, practical, technical and scientific curriculum. It is, I think, true that most European education from classical times has some social overtone to it: the notion of a totally self-contained knowledge serving only as an end in itself, though not infrequently evoked, has rarely been found in its purest form. European education, in general, is in some degree instrumental: Plato wished at the highest level to form philosophic beings as rulers, not hermits; scholastic training was not irrelevant to the lives of churchmen; humanists desired to affect conduct. The implicit practicality of the empirics hardly requires stress. It is perhaps the case that the cause of liberal education obtained more overt and explicit theoretical support during the nineteenth century than during the previous thousand years; this was partly a reaction against claims for excessive practicality, partly due to the view that the expansion and training of faculties was a good thing in itself and partly due to a horror of Victorian industrialisation: if this was what constituted practicality, let us avoid it, was the implication.

Grammar school education, as it has evolved in England, has always, in theory, been geared to these notions of liberalization (the same would be broadly true of the French *Lycée* and the German *Gymnasium*). I say 'in theory' because, clearly, a grammar school education, through its commitment to examination success, has also been the gateway to the professions and has therefore fulfilled a vocational function, even if an indirect one. Certainly it is a matter of degree; but the consensus among grammar school teachers has been that they have been concerned with the expansion of mind rather than vocational purposes, though their pupils have usually had a more instrumental view (cf. King, 1969; Stevens, 1960).

The modern defence of a liberal education has been sustained and articulated by certain philosophers of education — notably by Professor Paul Hirst. Professor Hirst makes it clear, in a discussion of the Harvard Report, *Liberal Education in a Free Society,* that he sees serious weaknesses in its attempt to define a liberal curriculum in terms of the characteristics of mind it attempts to foster (though I would add that the committee's justification of a liberal education in such terms indicates the persistence of the concern with mind) and prefers instead to place the emphasis on the 'forms of knowledge'. He points out that the psychological terms necessitated (e.g. 'effective thinking') can only be delineated through their publicly discussable features — i.e. through the forms of knowledge in terms of which they operate. Thus he considers the forms are 'logically prior' (1974, p. 35) and the psychological characteristics of mind only 'secondary and derivative'. Furthermore, he considers that to anchor curriculum in mind rather than in knowledge is to run the risk of broadening the concept of liberal education by including other aspects of personal development foreign to its original conception: 'On logical grounds, then, it would seem that a consistent concept of liberal education must be worked out fully in terms of the forms of knowledge', that is, 'complex ways of understanding *experience* which man has achieved, which are publicly specifiable and which are gained through learning' (p. 38; my italics). At the same time, he still considers that 'the achievement of knowledge is necessarily the development of mind', that 'to have "a rational mind" certainly implies experience structured under some form of conceptual scheme' (p. 39). Mind, then, plays an essential, if logically subordinate, part in his justification of liberal education as constituting 'in a very real sense the ultimate form of education' (pp. 42-3).

So the proposition with which I began this discussion of post-humanist developments, that under the influence of changes in epistemology and psychology the curriculum was conceived and supported in terms of some view of the interaction of mind and world ('knowledge' being in some sense a reflection of world), which includes the world of culture as well as of nature, receives contemporary theoretical justification. Undoubtedly there is a persistent tradition from at least the late seventeenth century which ties the development of the curriculum to notions of one sort or another concerning the functioning and nature of the mind on the one hand and to the concept of 'experience' (which is allowed to include experience of books as a still relevant, though certainly no longer exclusive, element) on the other.

But has not my exposition been too predominantly theoretical — revelatory indeed of the thought processes that have led to reform of the curriculum but too little attentive to those specifically social, political and economic factors which, in the end, have 'produced' the practical reforms?

XV

My reason for stressing the influence of educational theory on the development of the curriculum lies in the extent to which, in recent writings, the tendency has been to neglect the role of theory in preparing for change, and to emphasize, instead, a number of social, political and practical factors. Thus Dr Gordon and Professor

Lawton, in their *Curriculum Change in the Nineteenth and Twentieth Centuries,* refer to curriculum change as the 'result of complex patterns of interaction between influential individuals and general processes of social, political and economic change' (1978, p. 2). Clearly, in the actual *timing* of change, practicalities of this type play an important, indeed a crucial, role. Economic pressures (in terms of German industrial competition and all it entailed) undoubtedly played a fundamental part in the extension of the curriculum which, in various ways, was institutionalized towards the end of the nineteenth century and in the earlier years of the twentieth by the final acceptance of scientific subjects into the curriculum. This is not in dispute; in any case, theory is not a self-contained area, but is itself subject to social and cultural pressures. (Indeed, there are those who consider all thought processes as simply indicative of certain manifestations of the social and economic structure — they constitute epiphenomena. I shall have to say more about this argument in due course.)

Nevertheless, it is important, both within the context of this book and generally, not to underplay the role of theory. I am here concerned with the more profound cultural movements which have affected thinking about the curriculum at the deepest levels, not with the surface play of events; for it is only by revealing the fundamental nature of the contemporary curriculum, its relevance to and linkages with the basic categorisations in terms of which our society exists, that it is possible to clarify the real dilemmas of the curriculum in our times. Science has not simply become a subject on a time-table; it has affected our whole mode of thinking by introducing into human affairs a particular stress on contemporaneity. The nature of that thinking is revealed partly by assessing what it was reacting against in its initial phases and partly by gauging some of its effects in our thinking about the processes and incidence of education. And these are nowhere better revealed than in the historical evolution of the concern for 'things' that has been chronicled for us by the theorists.

Indeed, their long concern with the educative value of 'things' had carried out the essential preparatory work of reorientation long before social and practical changes made curriculum adjustment either essential or even feasible. Change institutionalized in the schools comes about, by and large, as a result of conscious decision — and much preparatory work in the consciousness of men is necessary before 'opinion' becomes sufficiently acclimatized to undertake the advocated reorientation, a fact that was explicitly recognized in the nineteenth century by advocates of science education.[2] The effect of theorists is normally indirect and long term — but it is none the'less effective for that. Rousseau, Pestalozzi and Froebel waited about a century and a half before they seriously and deeply affected our public system of education — but affect it, in the end, they did.

Furthermore, it should be realized that any *system* of education (even more especially one that has now become universal) is necessarily tempted to work at a highly abstract level. Unlike the education of the home, the great house or domestic apprenticeship, it must structure its requirements to cope with the large numbers and wide diversity of children it is forced to receive — it cannot be tailored to individual cases easily. It must assess what is to be considered important in general terms. The abstractness of theory, then, far from being a disadvantage, provides precisely those generalized recommendations which are expected to meet the nature of the case. The school must look to the needs of an overall training; as a bureaucratic entity it is doomed at least to a degree of abstraction. T. S. Eliot was right to identify contemporary education in these terms — but the necessity of becoming so is built into the universality of the requirement. It is no accident that, with the spread of education, theory proliferated — nor that the concrete actualities of human behaviour, still present in the humanist concern for words, have gradually been replaced by the abstractness of a concept like 'mind' as the guiding thread through the maze of prescriptions that have characterized this proliferation.

Finally, it can be said that there are a number of historian-sociologists who have charted some of the specific socio-historical factors determinative of particular curricular changes, and one hardly needs to add to them (e.g. Gordon and Lawton, 1978; Musgrave, 1968; etc.). Here I am concerned with identifying the movements of thought that have lain behind curriculum evolution in order to assess their implications for our present discontents. The strength of the scientific movement from the seventeenth century onwards was such that, at some stage, something must have focused curricular attention on it: the specific events that triggered off the changed balance of humanities and sciences is of local rather than fundamental interest.

XVI

What I have emphasized, then, has involved a profound reorientation of the whole nature of the curriculum from the time of the Renaissance. Initially, what was learned was geared to a moral purpose, for its subject matter was suffused with a morally didactic aim. Its central core was a literature, whether patristic or classical, and its essentially authoritative guidance was reflected in both the matter and manner of its content. Renaissance education sprang out of a clearly defined cultural context and was intended at once to 'liberalize' and guide the conduct and behaviour of a social and political elite. It was a total education, intended to encompass all aspects of the personality — mind, carriage, social behaviour and physical accomplishments, all informed at its most sophisticated with the 'grace' that constituted the ideal of courtly behaviour. Its main instrumentality was language — words; words used in the appreciation of their full denotative and conotative roles, encompassing both content and 'style'. Whether manifest in a more formal oratory or a more informal conversation it was directed to an amelioration of political or administrative life through its understanding of human nature and an utterance geared to a delight in elegance and sophistication; and this elegance was to suffuse the whole personality, so that bodily movement, gesture and tone of voice all added to the artistic impression created by content and choice of language. Indeed, it would not be outrageous to suggest that it involved, at its most refined, the creation of man as a work of art, realizing his 'inherent' nature through an assimilation of the highest ethical and cultural forms available to him through the internalization of a traditional culture. There are, in fact, broad analogies in the concepts deployed between theories of artistic creation and educational theories during this period.

But the knowledge implicit in a developing empiricism was essentially neutral in nature: it lacked moral content — it drew simply on an initial moral urge to discover 'truth' as that was reflected in the putative actualities of physical behaviour. Indeed, it arose out of a specific attempt, during the Enlightenment, to overthrow the traditional and initiate a fresh start, mind functioning autonomously apart from conventional 'encumbrances'. The transitional dilemmas are unconsciously revealed by Locke himself, who is traditional in his views of morals and manners but revolutionary in his conception of the autonomy of 'understanding'.[3] It is not only that orientation to a common world of experience has introduced a democratizing element — something different from the essentially elitist world of esoteric literatures — it is also that the role assigned to mind has made it peculiarly corrosive of traditional acceptances, requiring its own autonomy on the basis of 'evidence'. Though the humanities have continued to fulfil a moral purpose, the nature of that moral purpose has significantly altered. Literature to the humanist was the repository of a didactic wisdom, to be accepted on the authority of the ancients; literature to a modern teacher constitutes a scene of moral conflicts intended to assist moral insight on the basis of which the reader is helped to clarify the nature of his own moral conflicts: it serves the purpose of illumination, not didacticism. Much the same is true of religious instruction, the only obligatory section of the modern curriculum. The emphasis is increasingly on the need to teach *about* religion (indeed, about religions in a multi-racial society) and not to push the doctrines of any one belief.

The tendency, then, has been for thought to seek its own autonomy; morality necessarily enters into the relationships of a school — between teacher and taught and among the taught. But in general the curriculum no longer serves a *directly* moral end: it is to assist in the process by which children are helped to make up their own minds. Put another way, free-ranging thought is ideally to determine life, not imitation of superior models. The progress of knowledge has brought more and more areas of human existence to consciousness, to be rationally determined rather than accepted as habit or encouraged through imitation of pre-existing patterns of behaviour. Indeed it is the contention of many educational philosophers that such autonomy is an essential concomitant of morality itself — that choice constitutes a crucial element in any genuine system of ethics and that any suggestion of authoritative guidance would constitute 'indoctrination'. Thus the development of autonomy is seen as an essential feature of any sophisticated morality. The only restrictions arise out of the immaturity of the pupils — whose inability to handle moral concepts meaningfully below a certain age constitutes the sole grounds for authoritative intervention. Indeed, such immaturity is often considered the main justification for the imposition of a curriculum at all (as 'worth-while activities' and therefore subject to value discrimination) and only whilst choice in this area cannot be regarded as meaningful. ('Progressives', however, would claim somewhat differently, as we shall see.)

There is one developing feature of modern knowledge, however, which has militated against the width of curriculum here chronicled — and that can be referred to as its 'explosion'. Knowledge has extended so greatly that its sheer bulk imposes the necessity of specialization in ways that are at odds with general cultivation. It's not simply the social demand for expertise in limited fields; it's the fact that to grapple with any subject with due attention to its full *educative* possibilities increasingly necessitates concentration rather than diversification. The danger of general education has become superficiality and dilettantism; the danger of specialist education lies in its limitation of viewpoint and the inability to assess what is acquired in depth within a wider intellectual context. This constitutes one of the fundamental dilemmas of the elite curriculum in the modern world. The ideal of a wide-ranging intellect encounters the harsh realities implicit both in the constant growth of knowledge and in the development of a social structure that requires expertise rather than breadth of understanding for its implementation.

XVII

There is, however, one area where development has been severely limited: that of the fine arts — music, painting, sculpture, etc. Only poetry and drama — the latter traditionally treated as text rather than as potential performance — have become the concern of mainstream thinking on education. Among the humanists, Vittorino da Feltre placed some emphasis on aesthetic elements, especially music; and some introduction to the arts (especially music and dance) played a part in the training of the courtier — dance assisted deportment and hence fostered social graces. But in general what have come to be regarded as the fine arts were, in humanist days, still too closely associated with a labouring craft tradition to be rated highly in the curriculum. Only by the later Renaissance had they developed those intellectual and theoretical 'liberalizing' features that enabled them to be treated with respect as worthy of serious educational study — and, by then, they were to encounter the beginning of that hostility the 'empirics' showed to all artistic experience on the ground of its essentially 'fictional' nature. The arts tended, therefore, to suffer from a double disability — one social, the other intellectual: they were always in danger of being associated with the wrong social group (indeed, artists and craftsmen), and they were not regarded as serious contenders in the delineation of 'truth', which depended on empirical evidence.

So drawing, when allowed, tended to be advocated on the grounds of its social or military usefulness — it enabled one to record military installations or record a scene. It needed the romantics to stress the 'creative' values of arts and make important claims for the emotional benefits of forms of artistic education. It is undoubtedly one of the benefits of 'romantic', 'naturalistic' progressivism that in recent years much more emphasis has been placed on the arts. Again, theories relating to the mind — Freudian and *gestalt* — have played their parts in justifying attention to the arts. A good example of an important seminal work that draws on both is Herbert Read's *Education through Art* (1958). One of the difficulties, however, has been the naive notion, also encouraged by romantic progressivism, that 'creativity' was largely endogenous, a capacity with which a child was born and which needed only opportunity and encouragement rather than something on which to bite, whether technical or experiential. This, also, has tended to stultify progressive efforts to incorporate aesthetic elements into the curriculum — the consequent outpourings have been more remarkable for their becoming manifest than for their quality.

In general, however, the arts have had a low profile in the traditional grammar school curriculum; they have appeared as recreational extras — time-tabled, but generally regarded less seriously and with less time allocated than the humanities and sciences.

XVIII

This chapter has not been intended to provide a blow-by-blow account of how the modern curriculum has evolved out of the medieval and humanistic *trivium,* but rather to provide some insight into the fundamental principles making for change and how they have affected the character of the education provided. The changes have naturally reflected and been reflected in reorientations in society. The central concept of Renaissance education was 'imitation', implying a still backward looking society, hierarchical and therefore providing models of superiority with a view to exercising social power through persuasion; the concept still ideally predominant today is 'autonomy', signifying the freeing of mind from traditional social commitments, and the pursuit of its solitary cognitive path with a view to achieving moral independence and selling its acquired skills to the highest bidder. Both constitute superior forms of education — elitist would be today's description — and both reflect the natures of the disciplines that dominate their context: in the one case esoteric ancient literatures, in the other the openness of an advancing scientific investigation.

But, just as the former predominance passed away, so the current ideal of cognitive autonomy suffers a number of stresses and strains. There is, first, its extension to a total population following the introduction of universal education in the latter years of the nineteenth century; to what extent can it be regarded as within the cognitive grasp of all? Furthermore, it depends on a willingness to accept delayed satisfactions: a withdrawal from immediate practicality to foster the internalization of disciplines requiring mastery before application, a process that would seem to run counter to certain psychological principles of motivation which rely on interest and an immediate pragmatic application. Another aspect of this encounters 'socialization' as an aim. Finally, there are those who would see in knowledge, as at present constituted, only a means of political control, possessing no universal validity but reflecting the interests of the dominant class. In general, they reject cumulative notions of educational knowledge — which they identify with the reinforcement of the *status quo* — but see knowledge as an instrument of change, implying the simultaneous presence of reflection and action as a counter-blast to the 'symbolic violence' implicit in mainstream educational practice that fosters an oppressive politicized cultural hegemony. All these features imply a need to examine the challenges implicit in the common curriculum, progressivism and educational radicalism to the still dominant but much questioned ideal, 'liberal' model — and then to consider the internal stresses to which that model is itself subject. I shall concentrate my attention on the formal curriculum, deeming it of crucial importance in itself; aspects of the so-called 'hidden curriculum' will be implied rather than be the subject of an extended comment.

XIX

Before I turn to these matters, however, I must anticipate a further objection readers may wish to make against discussing the curriculum through the idealizations of theorists. Granting that these constitute models representative of particular historical articulations, would not their implementation reveal significant differences from the ideal in practice?

Of course, to some extent, this is bound to be the case. The threat to the humanist curriculum in practice was pedantry and mechanical reproduction; that to the present curriculum is transformation into examination fodder. But, in both cases, there were clearly successes and identifiable manifestations of the spirit intended. Humanist education, we know, helped to produce a Shakespeare and a Milton — the cases have been carefully documented (cf. p. 118 below); in grammar schools the forms of knowledge were transmitted in a way recognizably representative of a sought-for liberality. It was certainly not directed to specifically vocational ends.

We all know, in T. S. Eliot's words, that 'Between the idea/And the reality/Between the motion/And the act/Falls the Shadow'. Any actuality represents a travesty of an ideal; nevertheless, in any *generalized* comment on a state of affairs that exists in so very many separate institutions, it is only possible to proceed in terms of the ideas by which they are collectively activated, for individual comment is neither possible nor acceptable as representative. I believe my description of curriculum change to be broadly characteristic of what, in the fullness of time, has actually happened. I believe that in a book devoted, *in general,* to curriculum problems in the modern world it is only possible to approximate to the actualities of the situation by examining what men have thought they were doing. All men, after all, not only act but are influenced by conceptions of how they ought to act. In a highly self-conscious entity like the school, thought about the school must play an important and identifiable part; one gets as near as one can to its actual functioning if one considers how those thoughts operate and what tensions and conflicts they give rise to. For one comes to recognize those tensions and conflicts in the actual conduct of schools.

In any case, it would be absurd to deny that theoretical considerations, wisely deployed, can be highly revealing. Thus, for exemplary purposes only, I would adduce my own consideration of comprehensive education. Long before comprehensive schools actually began to appear in this country I raised certain important theoretical issues (including, for instance, the internal incoherence of their ideology) that led me to caution against their over-hasty introduction (cf. especially my *Education in an Industrial Society,* 1963). I believe that the concrete embodiment of the comprehensive idea has led precisely to those stresses and difficulties I forecast and that my caution has been fully justified in the event — and yet I had no English empirical evidence whatsoever to draw on. We really must get out of the way of thinking that it is impossible to analyse a project until the often dubious findings of some social scientists give us the go-ahead; and indeed, a powerful imagination geared to a sense of fundamental human realities is often a better guide than empirical findings based on an inadequate comprehension of the subtleties of situations. After all, social science like the computer can only reveal in accordance with the adequacy of its programming — and in a number of cases this leaves much to be desired.

NOTES

1. The words refer originally to a space where three or four streets meet.
2. Thus two pioneers of science education, Walter McLeod and Thomas Tate, agreed that 'Locke, Pestalozzi, and the advocates of object lessons were the true begetters of the movement, the progress of which could be traced through the work of reformers such as Wilderspin and Stow to the present day' (Layton, 1973, p. 123).
3. Cf. my study of Locke (Bantock 1980). Here will be found a much fuller treatment of some of the themes briefly noted in this chapter.

CHAPTER 2

Progressivism and the Curriculum

I

As indicated in the previous chapter, there is a sense in which a liberal education remains a superior education — one that involves effort without thought of immediate gain. Though science, at least in its initial phase, had clear democratic implications (its pursuit, in Bacon's words, was thought to 'level men's wits'), and certainly implied a common world of observation rather than an esoteric world of an arcane literature, yet nevertheless, as scientific knowledge advanced, it fostered its own forms of esotericism. The phase when humanists could also be scientists was gradually threatened as advancing knowledge in scientific and technical fields demanded increased specialization: our contemporary notion of a liberal education, indeed, has fostered at least some initiation into both the sciences and the humanities in the earlier years of schooling but during the twentieth century the tendency has been for specialization to begin sooner rather than later. The needs of professionalism, the social necessity for experts, the growth of social mobility and the emphasis on 'opportunity' have made 'liberalization' a more difficult curriculum policy to pursue. Liberal education gained in attractiveness when it was sustained by a particular sense of freedom from immediate vocational obligation: after all, its roots lay in the Greek notion of leisure. Always, in former emphases on liberal education, there has been the appreciation to fall back on that some knowledge is more worth having than others (the notion of hierarchy); and that which is most worth knowing is that which in some sense or other revealed a truth beyond daily exigencies.

However intellectually disreputable Plato's notion of the Forms may appear today, in an age demanding empirical verification, it was, nevertheless, a stimulus to a particular sort of social and intellectual involvement — as, for that matter, was the whole system of Christian theology and metaphysics. They encouraged aspiration and implied a standard beyond that of material need. They sustained a view of knowledge as constituting the aim and purpose of mind apart from the specific demand of practicalities (we have seen such a view at work in the 1904 Regulations).

But knowledge, of course, was an ambiguous concept — it could imply 'knowing how' as well as 'knowing that', knowledge as a tool rather than as an object of contemplation, for use rather than as a stored commodity. As hinted in the previous chapter, there were calls for 'relevance'; more, there were repercussions from the scientific study of man that fostered psychological emphases on the importance of motivation, revealed the crucial part in learning played by 'interest', asserted the growing need to meet the psychological principles implicit in development as well as the logical demands enshrined in subject-matter. Hence progressivism, which focused its gaze on the child, rather than on the knowledge he was to acquire.

Furthermore, if the study of mind and its psychological and epistemological dimensions produced mainstream thinking about the importance of knowledge and its forms, a 'many-sided interest' as the formative power in terms of which mind defined itself, alternative theses saw cognition as only an element in a complex that included social, emotional and physical factors. Especially did the identification of social elements tie in with the ideology of egalitarian democracy and a desired harmony of social relationships that would foster growth through participation in a more united and fraternal social order. The central tradition of educational thought tended to concentrate on mind as an autonomous factor seeking its ultimate realization through its identification with a knowledge isolated from the exigencies of the daily flux of events; progressives saw mind as essentially an offshoot of continual contact with daily events and the problems they posed. The division is, perhaps, too sharply drawn — but it highlights the very real differences implicit in the two approaches and enables us to begin an assessment of the implications for curriculum of the psychological and social factors emphasized by progressivism. As before, a historical approach will prove fruitful.

II

Progressivism can be regarded primarily — and indeed exclusively — as a methodology, a new way of accomplishing the traditional aims of cultural transmission by exploiting those psychological discoveries concerning optimum learning conditions. Indeed, as an umbrella term it covers so many meanings that there are certainly some people who would term themselves 'progressives' and whose aim is simply to achieve superior standards in the traditional curriculum by new means.

But no serious consideration of the practice of many of our 'progressives' or of the long history, stretching from at least the eighteenth century, of the development of 'progressive' ideas could avoid the truth that progressivism, both traditionally and contemporaneously, had very serious implications for the content of education. The situation can be more easily and comprehensively understood if I start by examining the inferences to be drawn from an examination of the work of two men both of whom have been regarded as the 'father' of progressive education and both of whom have contributed to a developing ambivalence over the content of education. Briefly, Rousseau, in the education of the younger Emile (in the part of *Emile* that has exerted most influence subsequently), asserted the superiority of nature to culture; John Dewey affirmed the claims of community in preference to the restrictions, as he saw them, of the academic. Both views involve versions of primitivism and both have had repercussions on our view of curriculum.

The most superficial reading of *Emile* will make clear its author's attachment to the concept of 'Nature'; but a moment's thought will also make it clear that the idea of nature is being used in a number of different ways. Two are important for my theme.

Human development is putatively governed by 'natural' laws analogous to those discovered to be controlling the material environment. At times Rousseau seems to suggest that these laws assert themselves in purely endogenous terms: 'The mind should be left undisturbed 'till its faculties have developed' (1943, p.57). Hence the apparent lifting of all cultural restraints. At other times it is appreciated that 'nature' can be assisted by human intervention: 'His sense experiences are the raw material of thought: they should therefore be presented to him in fitting order' (p. 31). This quotation not only implies the tutor's active interference but points to the *kind* of learning that Rousseau wishes to encourage. In reaction against the verbalism of Renaissance humanism Rousseau asserts the importance of 'things' over 'words'. This allies him with many other advanced thinkers of the time; but his way of achieving his ends goes beyond their recommendations. In brief, the aim is to turn the child into a discoverer, learning to correlate phenomena and acquire technical skills in a way that implies that he becomes the main agency in his own education; and he can do this because all learning dependent on human records (on literature, for instance) is postponed until later. Symptomatically Rousseau banishes books ('the scourge of childhood') except *Robinson Crusoe* — the handyman's guide to self-sufficiency. The study of the social and emotional arts is to be delayed until adolescence — by which time the child will have been protected against the ravages of social corruption and concessions may be made to social life. The essence of the early Emilean experience lies in an attempt to transcend history — history interpreted as the influences of family and the traditional humanistic culture of Europe — though a limited technical competence (which, of course, must have a social origin) is to be preserved. In place of ordered curriculum are substituted, as organizing principles, the shifting and sporadic demands of daily living — the *practical* exigencies of daily life — and such coherence as the environmental tinkerings of the tutor can indirectly introduce. The forces appealed to are psychological: 'childhood has its own ways of seeing, thinking and feeling' (p. 54). The importance of activity is stressed: 'children will always do anything that keeps them moving freely' (p. 105). Motivation is crucial: 'Present interest, that is the motive power, the only motive power that takes us far and safely' (p. 81). Above all, let Emile find out through direct contact, not through verbal explanations: 'Experience precedes instruction' (p. 29). The contrast with the humanists is complete. Attention is directed not to an historical wisdom encapsulated in a series of specific texts but to the contingencies of daily life in which it is assumed the tutor can, through the subtle presentation of specific experiences, educe the ability to collate the behaviour of phenomena meaningfully. In so far as it is possible to detect any structure in this early education it lies in the production of technico-scientific man, learning to control his environment at near subsistence level. Ideologically it has been affected in the need to cope with 'ordinary' children (as in Rousseau's Emile and Pestalozzi's orphans, Dewey's 'majority').

Not surprisingly there are strong egalitarian overtones in this education. A form of simple, comparatively primitive (*not* savage) life becomes the norm to be achieved, within which the child is to accomplish self-regulation and self-direction in an egalitarian rural community — this is thought to constitute a more 'natural' form of existence than that to be found in towns and cities, for 'Nature's characters alone are ineffaceable, and nature makes neither the prince, the rich man, nor the nobleman'; the normative overtones, rarely absent from Rousseau's use of the concept of Nature, are brought into play in order to persuade in a way that would cause a modern geneticist to raise his eyebrows at the implication intended. The same sleight of hand is used to blur reaction to the evaluative implications of 'needs' in the statement: 'natural needs are the same to all' (p. 157). As a creative principle 'Nature' (among other things) implies a degree of homogenization; it contributed greatly to the Enlightenment's anti-hierarchical stance and has entered into the fundamentals of political thinking down to our own day. Again, there are implications for the curriculum; manifestations of traditional or sophisticated culture are deprecated: 'Every one knows that the learned societies of Europe are mere schools of falsehood, and there are assuredly more mistaken notions in the Academy of Science than in the whole tribe of American Indians' (p. 167). Even as a young man, when it becomes necessary to introduce him to the social and moral world and, therefore, to what traditionally would have been categorized as humanistic studies, Emile is allowed to read the classics only on the grounds that they contain 'a certain simplicity of taste which goes straight to the heart' (p. 308), a finding that would have astonished the humanists. Modern productions are largely dismissed — as are modern sophisticated artistic tastes. It is not surprising that, some years ago, Sir Isaiah Berlin described Rousseau as the 'first militant low-brow in history'. In so far as any clear social integration is achieved, the preference for the simple rural existence persists — the 'patriarchal, rural life, the earliest life of man, the most peaceful, the most natural' (p. 438).

III

From here the story can be taken up by John Dewey. Dewey lies uneasily between a liberal, individualized past and a collectivist, homogenized future. Two elements in his thinking continue Rousseau's line of thought: his instrumentalism and his concern for 'democracy'. As an instrumentalist, Dewey, like Rousseau, saw knowledge as something for use, as an 'instrument' in the more effective control of the environment to serve man's purposes; it involved 'a change from knowing as an aesthetic enjoyment of the properties of nature regarded as a work of divine art, to knowing as a means of secular control' (Dewey, 1929, p. 100). This involved a development of Rousseau's principle of learning from the environment in order to cope with the exigencies of daily life: 'mere amassing of information apart from the direct interests of life makes mind wooden', he writes, in his own wooden way. And so he becomes the father (as Rousseau was the grandfather) of the 'project', the real life situation as the organizing principle in terms of which the logical development of subject matter is 'psychologized' (Dewey, n.d., p. 22) for the purpose of making it meaningful: 'The school must represent present life — life as real and vital to the child as that which he carries on in the home, in the neighbourhood, or on the playground' (Dewey, 1941, p. 6). Dewey's concern for democracy and its implications I shall reserve for the next chapter.

IV

So far I have alluded briefly, and in general terms, to the implications of these views of the founding fathers of progressivism for the content of education. It is now necessary to spell these hints out in much greater detail. Before I do so, however, there is one general point of great importance, concerning the whole orientation of the traditional education vis-à-vis the progressive.

As I have made clear earlier, the enterprise of traditional

'liberalizing' education was informed by conceptions of excellence, by the search for perfection, for the Idea in its highest form. Whether the aim is to produce the Philosopher-King (Plato), the Orator (Quintilian), the humanist Courtier (Castiglione) or the Autonomous Mind (initiated by Locke) — all, incidentally, intended to take an *active* part in affairs — in each case it is a notion of the Ideal type which exercises the controlling influence over the content of their education: 'It would be absurd to deny that a philosopher is a lover of truth and reality; or that his nature, as we have described it, is allied to perfection' (Plato). 'The Orator whom we are educating is the perfect orator, who can only be a good man' (Quintilian). 'I would like our game this evening to be this: that one of us should be chosen and given the task of depicting in words a perfect courtier' (Castiglione); and the tradition was carried on into the nineteenth century by Herbart, Arnold, Cardinal Newman and others. It is this 'vision of greatness' — in Whitehead's phrase — which has informed the determination of curriculum in the past; and, as the social role aimed at has been conceived of in its perfection, so the contributory activities, whether mental or physical, have been conceived of in their own specific perfections. Hence the frequent emphasis on 'imitation' — of the best models; and any 'usefulness' was to be informed by an antecedent liberalization. The autonomy of mind was, in fact, an autonomy from daily exigencies. In these ways, the accidental events of everyday life would be encountered by a mind already prepared to assess such accidents by reference to 'philosophic' principle and contextual significance, by a mind initiated into the circle of knowledge.

But the principle behind the progressive view of the curriculum is essentially that of the accidental; Rousseau wishes for an education that will be immediately useful — 'Life is the trade I would teach him' (1943, p. 9) — and the motivating force is provided by the incidents of daily existence: the activities of the gardener, a conjurer at a fair, a note from Emile's parents, an attempt to gather the cherries from the tree in the garden. Clearly Rousseau is still sustained by the Christian-humanist ethic — 'life' for him would not have included the activities of a Fagin — but his approach involved little ordered attempt to convey the structures of knowledge in a coherent fashion that fastened attention on the primary importance of mastering disciplines and their essential natures. And the same is true of the modern British primary school in its more progressive guise — as it is becoming of many middle and comprehensive schools. Temporary *interest* and immediate *need* are the guiding principles implicit in the attempt to 'psychologize' learning; hence the emphasis on motivation and endogenous development too easily fosters a magpie curriculum of bits and pieces, unrelated and ephemeral. In the interests of a temporary *relevance* a more permanent and deeper comprehension is often sacrificed.

Let us, with this indictment in mind, consider the current fashion for the interdisciplinary. Subject divisions are often dismissed as 'artificial', largely on the grounds that everyday living constantly involves the crossing and recrossing of subject boundaries and 'life as real as the home or the playground' is the object of our endeavour. But, of course, our 'living' is only interdisciplinary, as it were, in our moments of inattention and of imperfect consciousness. As soon as we focus our attention, seek to transcend the often mindless play of our daily existence, we enter an essentially specialized world. That building is a certain shape — what is the meaning of that shape, of the way the space has been deployed? Only a knowledge of architecture in its central concern with mass, space and line can provide the answer. A study of 'Our Town' (a popular subject) involves historical, economic, geographical features (among others) that, to take on significance beyond the most superficial, imply some degree of inwardness with the concepts and developments of the various subject fields involved; otherwise all that occurs is a meaningless copying from books and authorities (a not infrequent manifestation, it can be said), in undifferentiated enthusiasm.

The error implicit in an exclusive diet of this sort of thing lies in its haphazardness — and its subjectivity. It is to see the world as an appendage of self, without a meaning to be sought or guessed at apart from the meaning temporarily assigned in relation to one's immediate interests; it marks a failure to appreciate the integrity of the other, of what lies outside the self. All action, of course, is personal action and depends in the last resort on the responsibility of the self. But that self, to be wisely formed, must display some humility before the achievements of other selves, which is what is implied by a culture, and which it is the business of education to transmit. The danger of an education based totally on imitation is, of course, atrophy; the danger of an education based on novelty, the 'dominance of the foreground' as Santayana puts it, and immediacy is instability and parochialism, with the eccentricities, and worse, that accompany these conditions.

As a child, I was brought up in a way that would currently seem barbaric — with an almost exclusive emphasis on rote learning. Between the ages of five and ten, I learnt chunks of the Bible, gobbets of Shakespeare, fifty spelling words a week, the names of the kings and queens of England and the chief battles, the names of county towns, chief manufactures, capes, bays, isthmuses, rivers — sometimes in blank incomprehension. (Never tell a child what he cannot understand, advised Rousseau; cf. 1943, p. 76). I have forgotten much of this — but I have not forgotten the lesson it implied: that the world, physical and cultural, existed as an entity apart from myself and that if I wished to learn about it I must come to terms with its existence. The famous remark in the Primary School Report of 1931 perpetuates a false dichotomy: 'the curriculum is to be thought of in terms of activity and experience rather than of knowledge to be acquired and facts to be stored.' Knowledge, as I have tried to indicate above, is an essential part of experience: mind is selective and left to itself only focuses meaningfully on what it already knows about.

I am far from saying that occasional projects of an interdisciplinary nature should not be undertaken; but it should be realized that even their value as stimuli is limited to an essentially restricted attraction unless the ephemeral configurations of daily existence are informed by a deeper understanding of the parts that are brought into temporary contiguity in the project — and that have been studied as 'subjects'. For 'subjects' are precisely ways in which the incoherence of everyday experience is made meaningful, broken down into its constituent elements and illumined by study in depth. Such study is not to be dismissed as artificial but is an essential element in that very comprehension of the foreground the progressives wish to promote.

Furthermore, it is a psychological error to think that even young children are attracted only by the immediate — the assumption being that their world is bound in by the scope of their sense experiences and their present, and often temporary, 'interests'. In contradistinction to Rousseau's analysis of La Fontaine's fable of the 'Fox and the Crow', with its emphasis on the scientific inaccuracy of the elements of the fable, Coleridge urged the need for the remote and the imaginative:

For from my early reading of fairy tales and genii, etc. etc. my mind had been habituated *to the Vast,* and I never regarded *my senses* in any way as the criteria of my belief. I regulated all my creeds by my conceptions, not by my *sight,* even at that age . . . I have known some who have been *rationally* educated, as it is styled. They were marked by a microscopic acuteness, but when they looked at great things, all became a blank and they saw nothing, and denied (very illogically) that anything could be seen . . . [1933, p. 532]

Even very young children appreciate some amplification of their surroundings. The theory behind a recent set of readers for young children, Leila Berg's *Nippers,* is that children appreciate the familiar and are at home among the actualities of language and sights assumed to belong to their everyday life. But many find it embarrassing to read out loud: 'Cor, don't it pong', which represents a degeneration into a patronizing uncouthness, and are bored with the mundaneness. They much prefer the 'unreality' of Sheila McCullogh's charming imagination or Dr Seuss's *A Cat in the Hat.*

The argument in favour of the exploitation of the immediate and the everyday in the name of stimulation and interest would seem to be most compelling at the younger ages, when children are, arguably, in the terminology of Piaget, at the level of 'concrete operations' and need the stimulus of the actual. What I have tried to show is that, even at this age, such principles governing the content of education should be treated with some caution as, at best, limited guides — limited both in the way in which sense experience itself is a limited principle to guide curricular choice and also in the way in which this is meaningless unless it is enforced by comprehension of significance — and significance is not a characteristic of surface. For the criticisms offered concerning the revised content of primary school work apply with even greater force at the secondary level — particularly where able children are concerned; as the capacity for abstraction increases, the excuse of concreteness no longer applies with the same force. Those who are ready for study in depth no longer require the titillations of immediacy as motivation.

As an example, let us see how 'relevance' works in relation to the teaching of a specific subject at secondary level — English. The traditional emphasis stressed, among other factors, the centrality of literature; it was not always well taught, but it constituted an attempt to grapple with the language at its finest points of excellence. Recently, the centrality of literature has been under attack. Drama has become spontaneous, 'active' drama revealing, too often, little other than the linguistic and histrionic impoverishment of the children creating it. Such literature as has survived has become mainly contemporary and often radical, necessitating, in many cases, the study of inferior texts which an earlier age would, at best, have prescribed for private reading. The progressive emphasis on either endogenous creativity (undisciplined by true familiarity with the language of greatness) or social relevance (applying the human reductiveness characteristic of much of the contemporary) has replaced an earlier concern for quality. Where language is concerned, 'middle-class' speech structures are being attacked in favour of 'everyday' speech. 'A new respect for everyday language is needed', writes Miss Nancy Martin in one of a series of articles published in *The Times Educational Supplement* (17 May 1974), the net effect of which (despite occasional disclaimers) is to deprecate the structures of educated speech in favour of the putative superior 'expressiveness' of the everyday. One does not need to be wedded to the turgidity of *some* school writing not to see the dangers of this — with its implied cult of an unregenerate and surface expressiveness. It is the same attitude that defends the introduction of 'pop' into the schools.

V

The dangers, then, of progressivism and its implications for the curriculum lie in the direction of fragmentation and trivialization. One can see that the school is in a genuine dilemma: following the introduction of universal schooling it has become necessary to adjust 'meaning' to a total population, and to teach as equals a secondary school intake some of whom are ill-adjusted to the demands of the traditional academic curriculum. To educate is to transmit meaning; and the development of meaning implies the ability to make finer and finer discriminations in languages (whether verbal or otherwise) of ever-increasing complexity and precision. The desire for equalization, one of the profound urges of the age, encounters, at some stage and with some pupils, the, at least apparent, limitations of their ability to grasp. Implicit in the notion of the forms of knowledge and the conceptual schemes within which they become manifest, is the need to cope with ever greater sophistication and, usually, abstraction.

The naive faith of the Enlightenment thinkers in the power of education (through the formation of the 'correct' associations or whatever) encounters the stubborn resistance of minds apparently unable to cope. The crisis of twentieth-century education is, at bottom, not a crisis of organization but one of content, of curriculum, of the nature of the meanings one seeks to transmit. The implied recognition of this has fostered, in view of the new audience for learning, the cult of immediacy and 'relevance' just chronicled. Behind this lies the attempt to preserve an equivalence of experience — manifest as a common curriculum — throughout the whole school population. This is where Dewey's views on democracy become revealing and it is with those I will begin a consideration of attempts to preserve a common curriculum in the next chapter.

CHAPTER 3

The Common Curriculum

I

The notion of a common curriculum, the more precise implementation of which has been highlighted by the move towards comprehensive education and the support this has evoked for the notion of a common experience in tune with its democratic, social aspirations, is merely the latest in a whole series of assimilations, organizational as well as intellectual, as egalitarian pressures have grown. Crucial in the development of equality was the increasing atomization of the individual implicit in the eighteenth-century Enlightenment's repudiation of accepted social and religious forms and the consequent attribution of a basic uniformity to the beings freed from traditional patterns of hierarchy. It is indeed ironic that, at the very moment of the coming of industrialization and its need for a highly differentiated and expert work force of technical and bureaucratic trained management recruited on a basis of talent, other forces implicit in the reduction of phenomena to uniform regularities characterising the new scientific outlook should have encouraged the notion of *human* uniformity. Social 'need' and ideological commitment, pulling in different directions, have thus lived in uneasy partnership for the last two hundred years, the former spawning the notion of equality of opportunity (to become unequal) and the other equality of outcome. What is even more remarkable is the persistence, and even development, of the latter notion in an era marked by such increased appeal to empirical fact — when the facts staring one in the face would seem to point to inequality of endowment.

There are, of course, few, if any, who actually expect immediate equalization in achievement; the ideal appears in assumptions about differentiation being produced by environmental and educational inequalities, in resistance to hereditarian notions, appeal to revised methodologies, claims for positive discrimination in the treatment of the under-achievers — and, above all, in the dogmatism of the common curriculum.

Where the curriculum is concerned, there are two broad approaches: one is the offshoot of the progressive attitude examined in the last chapter, the other accepts a more conventional, traditional view. The former advocacy rests on its transformation into specifically social terms, so that the integrating factor is not the logically developed subject-matter of a specific discipline, but some sort of configuration devised from the common *social* life of the participants exploited in a way that permits learning involvement by the group and at the same time directs its members to the elucidation of a common meaning. Put another way, the project is intended to have a socially ideological as well as an academic function, both through its form of organization and in its content. The person who best reveals the underlying assumptions of this orientation is Dewey, the implications of whose 'democratic' aspirations we now need to consider.

By 'democracy' Dewey implied more than a form of government; in essence it constituted a type of community relationship — and, most important for its implications for curriculum, the notion invaded the very concept of 'meaning' itself. It was not only a question of 'associated living' and 'freer interaction between social groups'; it was also a matter of the homogenization of significance in communication. William Blake (not exactly an Establishment figure) had reasserted the significance of individual experience, as against the unifying tendencies of the philosophy of the Enlightenment, with its conception of an abstract 'humanity' manifest as homogenized units, with his assertion 'A fool *sees* not the same tree that a wise man sees' (my italics); in contradistinction Dewey defines his social groups in terms of each individual's acceptance of a common *meaning*: 'to have the same ideas about things which others have, to be like-minded with them, and thus to be really members of a social group, is therefore to attach the same meanings to things and to acts which others attach' (1921, p. 36). For Dewey it is the *egalitarian* social situation which provides the great tool of the educator: 'In social situations the young have to refer their way of acting to what others are doing and make it fit in. *This directs their action to a common*

*result, and gives an understanding common to the participants. For
all mean the same thing, even when performing different acts'* (p. 47;
my italics). This common understanding of the means and ends of
action is the essence of social control. However unwittingly — and
one must surely acquit Dewey of *intent* — he had taken a long step
on the road to George Orwell's *1984,* where all meaning is the same
meaning, imposed by the Party ('War is Peace, Freedom is Slavery,
Ignorance is Strength').

In essence, we have here the fundamental *social* argument in
favour of comprehensive schooling — its putative power as an
instrument of social cohesion and even control. A powerful element
in the comprehensive lobby sees it as a vehicle of social justice and as
a means of doing away with what is regarded as a damaging
'divisiveness' in our society. For such people equality of *opportunity*
is not enough — we should seek (if necessary by 'positive
discrimination' in favour of the under-achiever) equality of *outcome.*
Dewey's views on 'meaning' represent the ultimate in that direction.

But these aspirations should not be dismissed as the pipe-dreams
of an outdated theorist. When he was Secretary of State the former
socialist Mr Reg Prentice favoured 'an element of positive
discrimination in favour of disadvantaged children' (cf. *Times* 5
September 1974). Professor Halsey has revealed a similar concern
on the grounds that 'where social or ethnic groups have unequal
average educational attainments compared to other groups there has
been social injustice' (cf. *Times Higher Educational Supplement* 22
December 1972). What has been largely talk in England has been
implemented by the United States. In an article in *New Society* (22
January 1976) Professor Nathan Glazer indicates that 'For ten years
America has drifted away from the principle of equal opportunity . . .
and into policies of statistical parity for ethnic groups in employment,
housing and education'. The notion of 'affirmative discrimination' in
his view had engendered 'individual injustices . . . ethnic rancour and
the imposition of a lower degree of competence in jobs at all levels'.

Dewey, indeed, is anti-elitist both in his view of the content of
education and in his conception of the personality structure that he
intends to emerge from participation. He aims at the breaking down
of 'those barriers of class, race, and national territory which kept
men from perceiving the full import of their activity' (1921, p. 101).
The traditional 'liberal' autonomous conception of the personality he
dismisses in these terms:

To set up an external aim strengthens by reaction the false conception of culture which identifies it with something purely 'inner'. And the idea of perfecting an 'inner' personality is a sure sign of social divisions. What is called inner is simply that which does not connect with others — which is not capable of free and full communication. [p. 143]

The implication for curriculum is twofold: 'The learning in school should be continuous with that out of school'; this necessitates, among other things, an anti-historical spirit, lest the learner should 'feel more at home in the life of other days than in his own'. Meaning is, after all, primarily social meaning, involving 'a context of work and play in association with others'. 'In place of a school set apart from life as a place for learning lessons, we have a miniature social group in which study and growth are incidents of present shared experience' (p. 416). Hence 'The scheme of a curriculum must take account of the adaptation of studies to the need of the existing community life; it must select with the intention of improving the life we live in common so that the future shall be better than the past' (p. 225). Here, then, we have the subordination of the 'liberal' curriculum to frankly socio-political ends, the production of a community life of a particular sort. Especially noteworthy are the hostility to individualism and the study of the past. Instead we are offered a pervasive stress on the present and an implied cultural homogenization in terms of a common social experience.

II

This concern for cultural homogenization as an essential element in social democratic consensus and harmonization leads Dewey to value considerations that have deeply affected current arguments concerning, and practice within, the comprehensive school. He has both emphasized the primary value of the experiences open to the widest number and at the same time denied the possibility of any discrimination on the grounds of intrinsic value as between different areas of subject-matter. Thus he asserts that 'the curriculum must be planned with reference to placing essentials first, and refinements second. The things which are socially most fundamental, that is, which have to do with the experiences in which the widest groups share, are the essentials' (p. 225). At the same time he also asserts that:

> We cannot establish a hierarchy of values among studies. It is futile to attempt to arrange them in an order, beginning with one being least worth and going on to that of maximum value. In so far as any study has a unique or irreplaceable function, in so far as it makes a characteristic enrichment of life, its worth is intrinsic or incomparable. [p. 281]

The contradiction between 'first' and 'second' in the first quotation vis-à-vis the categorical refusal in the second to arrange in any order hardly requires comment. Yet it is precisely this covert approach of mediocritization in terms of appeal to the widest numbers, combined with an overt uncertainty about value discriminations, which has come to characterize comprehensive education in various countries today.

The comprehensive undertaking is the product of two contrary impulses, one seeking greater equality of *opportunity,* the other implying greater equality of *outcome.* Inefficiencies of selection in England at 11+ (and, despite the care taken, no-one can refuse to admit such inefficiencies, though in the opinion of the National Foundation for Educational Research they can be reduced to about 10 per cent of wrong placements) led to the belief that there was a hidden reservoir of talent currently depressed by the low status of the secondary modern school. Remove the stigma of that institution by grouping all in the same school and late developers would blossom, anomalies concerning percentage allocations to grammar schools would be ironed out, and a more equal opportunity would be afforded to all to become unequal. But there is a powerful body of comprehensive opinion which emphasized the social, 'democratic' implications of the single school. The mixture of different social classes within the same institution would promote mutual under-standing and sympathy. This necessitated the submission of all to a similar regimen or, in order to allow for the differences in capacity for learning that undoubtedly manifest themselves, promoted a value relativism, reminiscent of Dewey's refusal to discriminate between activities, which allocated an equivalent worth to the university scholar and the champion swimmer. (That animals can swim but cannot operate within human symbolic systems, and therefore that swimming constituted a relatively low grade activity, escaped notice.)

But the long-range effort was to promote equality of *outcome,* on the grounds that current deficiencies among certain sections of the school population were due, not to 'innate' or irreducible differences of ability but to the accident of family background and impoverished upbringing. Hence support for the common curriculum has become institutionalized.

III

Here, indeed, we have one complex of arguments and inferences intended to sustain a common curriculum: it is explicitly conceived of as serving a social purpose and as helping to induce a particular sort of community life; and undoubtedly such views lie behind some very specific curricular decisions which are taken in our comprehensive schools. The classics are out on the grounds of their irrelevance to the 'needs' of the majority; literature is modern literature because of its apparent relevance to contemporary conditions; social studies naturally serve a socializing purpose; the humanities project enables a utilization of knowledge in terms of its applicability to specific social problems; non-streaming assists intercommunication at different intellectual and social levels, which comes to be an acceptable part of the 'hidden' curriculum; subject 'barriers' are broken down and work organized on topic bases for reasons already divulged and discussed. Dewey's indignation against the historical is sustained in a school that exists not two miles from where I am working — where any engagement with pre-twentieth century material is only supported as having contemporary relevance.

I shall examine, in the next chapter, another important manifestation of much the same spirit of socialization — the cult of a putative working-class culture and the deprecation of the 'middle classes',[1] arising out of Dewey's insistence on the priority of majority interests and his unwillingness to consider value discrimination in other terms. But an admirable example of the way which, in the comprehensive school, immediately appealing trivialisations put at risk able children's commitments to more demanding — and ultimately more rewarding — disciplines, comes to hand in this specific example from a northern English school:

At Harpurhey [a comprehensive high school for 1100 girls in north-east Manchester] the academic groups have complained at not having the same opportunities [as less able groups]. . . This flattering jealousy is getting a special boost from the experimental 'Charm course' (hair-dressing, clothes, make-up, poise, diet, etc.) . . . The phenomenon was already observable during the North-West project trials [for R.S.L.A. pupils] . . . There was quite a feeling all through the trials by the more able children that they were being deprived. ['Business as usual' . . ., 1974]

One should hardly be surprised at such instances. A hundred years ago Matthew Arnold pointed to the problem, in an evolving Swiss democracy, of keeping up 'superiorities'. The effort that any sustained form of civilized life demands is difficult enough in a society that explicitly recognizes and rewards such manifestations; where there are powerful forces concerned to bring effort, restraint and delayed satisfaction into disrepute, the temptations of indulgence become for many overwhelming. We have yet to count the cultural cost of the socialized comprehensive school and its encouragement and endorsement of mass interests in pop music, charm schools and the like. And it is all implicit in Dewey's attack on historical tradition and, by implication, minority cultural interests.

IV

Here, then, advocacy of 'commonness' reinforces those aspects of trivialization and mediocratization of school curricular experience already foreshadowed in other manifestations of progressivism examined in the last chapter.

We are now perhaps in a position to see the contemporary dangers posed historically by Rousseau's insistence on nature and Dewey's on socialization. Both constitute forms of threat to traditional culture by way of an over-attention to the trivia of daily existence — whether social or 'natural'; both imply the immediate, the foreground, an attenuated sense of relevance as the criterion of judgement; both imply a restless, unfocused attention, failing to appreciate that each manifestation of daily life, properly conceived, belongs to a context that transcends the immediate, and finds its meaning only in a memory that is not present or in a configuration that transcends the incidental. The essential contrast between the old and the new education can be expressed in this way. The old has been based on the autonomy of the culture as something to be come to terms with, submitted to and grappled with in its own terms; the new, whether at the behest of 'nature' or the collectivity, implies all the restrictiveness of immediate relevance; this 'relevance' and its implications for content, may be controlled either by the accidents of personal viewpoint and immediate whim or the homogenization implied by majority commitment. The current thinness of much modern artistic culture, for instance, can be explained in terms of the personal impoverishment implied in theories that are either excessively individual or excessively social in their outlook. In art, action painting and Soviet realism both display a characteristic impoverishment, one through excessive idiosyncrasy, the other through excessive conventionality. The schools currently reflect an analogous impoverishment as a result of the impact of progressivism in its individual or social manifestations, for these are, after all, only the pedagogic manifestations of a general cultural debilitation. The concern for 'nature' — in its several significances — or for the collectivity in education are merely particular instances of a general movement towards reductionism and homogenization that constitute the present threat to the future of European culture in a mass age. What has taken place is a shift in man's metaphysical image of himself — from a self that has to be made, 'fashioned', to a self that simply has to be expressed. Rousseau's assertion of the importance of childhood as a state in its own right, rather than as a potential for actualization, marks — paradoxically — a diminution of childhood itself.

V

However, one also finds 'liberal' educationists pressing the claims of a common curriculum in ways that are intended to stress, not socialization, but liberal, individual 'autonomy'. Though concerned to support 'democratic' aspirations, implementation would protect the traditional 'forms of knowledge' — albeit with minor modifications as between theorists; so the orientation is clearly liberal-atomistic rather than socialized-collectivist. The most interesting and thorough philosophical study intended to support this view of the common curriculum, Mr J. P. White's *Towards a Compulsory Curriculum,* stresses its individual rather than its social implications. Indeed, he himself refers, in a bibliographical note, to the need for 'a necessary corrective to the individualistic point of view [I] adopted in most of this book' (1973, p. 108) in urging us to read Herbart to supply a morally integrative antidote; though he does also briefly note the need for some such corrective at several points in the text of his book.

Mr White is concerned fundamentally with 'rational educational planning'; and with that in mind he evokes the principle that 'any rational educational system must at least have the pupil's good in mind' (p. 8). In talking about goods he distinguishes between intrinsic and extrinsic ones. He finds himself unable to justify the pursuit of the arts and sciences on intrinsic grounds but argues that they can be shown to be educationally valuable. This being the case, it now becomes important to decide whether the imposition of these disciplines can be justified. He argues that children should be placed in a position where they can make responsible choices for their future, otherwise harm may occur. In this way, it is 'right to make [them] unfree now so as to give [them] as much autonomy as possible later on' (p. 22), and thus justifies compulsion. At the same time he is careful to distinguish 'autonomy' as an educational outcome from autonomy as an ideal of life: 'Autonomy, we might say, is a "must" if we are looking at what is educationally worth while; what is worth while in itself as an ideal of life is quite another question' (p. 23).

Autonomy is thus an instrumental, not an intrinsic end; it must include the right to choose slavery if, having encompassed the possible choices, the pupil in the end so decides. Nevertheless it is clear that, educationally speaking, this aim of autonomy constitutes a very different purpose from the socialization that sustains Dewey's similar support for commonness of provision. Dewey's aim constitutes an end in itself, an induction into a specific form of life — the 'democratic'; White sees his educational purpose as a 'freeing' of the individual so that he can make responsible choices for himself. Both, certainly, define a certain 'basic minimum' of curriculum exposure: Dewey through his socialized curriculum in order that a child may become inducted into a desirable way of life; White through a common core curriculum in order that a child shall be free to choose what he wants. Dewey's comes perilously near to constituting a form of imposed collectivisation; White opts for what Professor Cranston has termed 'compulsory rational freedom' — the child is to be forced to be free to choose.

Thus White's argument in favour of an imposed common curriculum arises out of the negative position that not to introduce a child compulsorily to certain categories of activities is to harm him by denying him certain future possibilities of choice. Dewey's argument in favour of his socialized activities is the positive one that they will help to produce the sort of personality structure and socially oriented individual he considers desirable. Mr White educes the liberal position that an individual should be so educated as to be 'free' to make his own choices, Dewey the collectivist view that the individual should be 'encouraged' to fit into a certain social pattern. (Despite Dewey's disclaimer that the teacher is not there 'to impose certain ideas or to form certain habits in the child, but is there as a member of the community to select the influences which shall affect the child and to assist him in properly responding to these influences' (1941, p. 8), a disclaimer that seems to give the lie to any charge of collectivization — in fact, the crux of the matter relates to the emphasis to be given to 'properly' and 'select', especially the former. What happens if the child fails to live up to expectations in terms of propriety? That there are still 'liberal' elements in Dewey is undeniable; that the general orientation of his thought is collectivist seems to me equally undeniable.)

Mr White divides the various aspects of the curriculum into two categories: those where 'no understanding of what it is to want X is logically possible without engaging in X'; the other where 'Some understanding of what it is to want X is logically possible without engaging in X' (1973, p. 26). Examples of the first include linguistic communication, mathematics, the (exact) physical sciences; of the latter, speaking a foreign language, cricket, cooking and climbing mountains. The activities belonging to the first category Mr White wishes to make compulsory, to form the basis of his common curriculum to which he assigns half the teaching time. Though it is possible to quarrel with Mr White's categorization of the two sorts of activities, it should be emphasized that his views are put forward undogmatically; he allows for the possibility of error. Of more

fundamental importance is Mr White's commitment to the principle
of liberty: 'We simply have no right to make children learn things for
inadequate reasons' (p. 41); he finds it necessary to establish, at
some length, that 'The principle of liberty may be over-ridden . . . to
prevent harm both to the pupils themselves and to men in general'
(p. 35).

Though it is perhaps expressed in a philosophically more
fashionable language I can see little in this that would quarrel with
my own position as expressed nearly thirty years ago in *Freedom
and Authority in Education,* where I argued the general need for
authoritative intervention in order to free children within certain
disciplines so that they can make responsible choices. As I put it: 'For
by the light of nature a child knows neither what he wants to do nor
— as important — does he know what he doesn't want to do' (1965,
p. 190). Allowing for differences in terminology, Mr White's starting
position and up to a point his conclusions tally with my own. A case
for certain interferences with 'liberty' seems to be unassailable where
children are concerned. After all, children's liberty has already been
interfered with — they have to go to school. In these circumstances,
deciding not to introduce them to certain subjects is just as much in
need of ethical justification as the imposition of compulsion in
certain areas — the logic of the school situation necessitates value
decisions concerning what not to teach as well as what to teach.

So Mr White establishes the justification of compulsion for the
first category of subjects — those that cannot be understood without
engagement. Here at least there is no 'progressive' concern for
'interest', motivation or psychological capacity; the prescription rests
— until a final argument to be considered shortly — on the
educational value of the subjects involved and their unintelligibility
without some commitment.

I disagree with Mr White, however, over the issue of the viability
and intelligibility of some of his chosen compulsory subjects for
certain children. It is noticeable that his aspirations become ever
more abstract. We begin with the identification of those subject
areas which must be part of the common curriculum because it is not
possible to understand their nature without some participation; from
there, on the grounds that 'it is not enough to equip pupils with a
broad understanding of wants which may figure as items in a way of
life, for ways of life themselves may be among the things which men
may want' (White, 1973, p. 43), it becomes necessary 'to finish their

education with an understanding of the many different ways of life which they and others may pursue' (pp. 43-4) — as guiding principles in terms of which men in different ways may conduct themselves. This movement towards ever higher levels of abstraction is summarized: 'Beginning with understanding items of a very particular sort, isolable activities, we moved on to understanding whole ways of life and thence to the integration of both types of understanding in the construction of a way of life from a self-regarding and finally from a universalistic moral viewpoint.'

It is little wonder that he describes this as a 'movement from particularity to wider and wider levels of generality' (p. 54). We have a typically rationalist construction unchecked by any empirical awareness of the concrete actualities that many teachers have to face. It reminds one irresistibly of a comment by W. B. Yeats on a play by Shaw: 'It seemed to me inorganic logical straightness and not the crooked road of life' (1926, p. 348). Only once, before his last chapter, does he introduce questions of possible psychological limitation; and here he prefaces his discussion by indicating that the assumption that 'children . . . have achievement potential . . . is not something that can be taken for granted . . . It is not at all clear, at least for normal children, that there are ceilings of general ability or of specialized ability in the different curriculum areas, beyond which they cannot go' (White, 1973, p. 65). His discussions on basic minima of content are vague in the extreme — it is in pursuit of his principle of liberty rather than with any sense of psychological limitation that he concedes that 'children should be obliged to study as little as possible' (p. 67).

It is difficult to believe, however, that Mr White is being serious when he suggests that there may be *no* ceilings. And indeed, later, in an attack on a paper of my own, Mr White goes so far as to concede that 'one could never show that someone had no ceiling'. He then argues that my own belief in 'the ineluctable differences in mental capacity' as between children is not a rational belief; instead, he identifies it as an article of faith (p. 99). But as we can, according to Mr White, neither prove nor disprove that children have differences in innate mental capacity, the only way in which we can proceed is on such evidence as we have; for when questions of a common submission to intellectual disciplines for all children are raised, the question as to whether all, some, or a few are likely to be able to cope cannot be avoided. If a man has no eyes it is not sensible to ask him to look. The undoubted empirical fact that children differ enormously in achievement may have more than one explanation: Mr White puts his trust in the belief in inefficient methodology on the part of teachers; but as he has had to admit that the question of innateness can never be tested, he can never be sure whether it is innateness or methodology that is at fault. Thus, when a child has difficulties over mathematical problems and he is faced with explanations in terms of either innateness or faulty methodology, Mr White's statement that 'There is good reason to prefer the latter alternative' (p. 98) on the grounds of the child's previous achievements in the field constitutes simply a statement of faith that this latest blockage does not mark the ceiling of the child's capacity. If I am to be taken to task on the grounds that verification of ceilings is not possible, Mr White must accept a similar rebuke because of his admission that falsification is equally impossible.

The fact of the matter is that both of us proceed *ultimately* on the basis of 'faith'. At one stage Mr White concedes that my particular faith may be — sometimes — justified, for he admits that 'Some self-styled environmentalists go too far in asserting that environmental improvements can bring all children up to the same intellectual level, i.e. that there are no insuperable barriers blocking some children's progress' (p. 99); if they 'go too far' then Mr White is here explicitly conceding the possibility of 'ceiling'. But apart from Mr White's contradictoriness in argument, in any situation of the kind where *certainty* can never be attained and yet when decisions have to be taken, it is necessary to proceed on those grounds that can be defended rationally as pertaining to the nature of the case. To expect *proof,* indeed, in such circumstances would be irrational, for to predict the future development of anything as complex as a child with absolute assurance is impossible. All one can do in such circumstances is to proceed responsibly, adducing such evidence as is available. Mr White speaks as if 'faith' necessarily lacks rational support; but there are many degrees between nescience and proof and, traditionally, even faith has usually been built on more than prejudice or irrational belief — as Aquinas and Newman bear witness. As Mr White admits (a) by implication that all children cannot be brought to the same level, (b) that the question of ceiling is neither falsifiable nor verifiable, the possibility of evidence for 'ineluctable differences' must at least be allowed to remain open.

I would not accept, then, that Mr White has made out an

unanswerable case for a common curriculum; and indeed it seems to me that there are perfectly reasonable grounds for advocating an alternative curriculum for the less able children. In the process of doing so I shall refer back once more to Mr White's point about 'faith' with a view to establishing that there are indeed very good reasons (which *necessarily* cannot, in the nature of the case, be said to constitute *proof*) for believing that some children are unable to encompass, in any meaningful way, the abstractions necessary for Mr White's common curriculum and that they would benefit more from alternative offerings.

But, first, it is necessary to consider the alternative offerings of certain radical thinkers. Interestingly, they appear to concede my case for an alternative rather than a common curriculum — but in terms that I find totally unacceptable.

NOTE

1. The term 'middle class' nowadays tends to be used to refer, not to Matthew Arnold's Philistines but to the upholders of 'middle-class' culture, which, by the left, is equated with high culture. Clearly 'middle-class' culture is much more complex than this, for it necessarily embraces what was traditionally regarded as 'middle brow' culture, which was to be carefully distinguished from 'highbrow' manifestations. In general, however, to avoid confusion I have accepted the attribution of 'highbrow' virtues to the middle classes and use the term with that in mind.

CHAPTER 4

Radical Views

I

I shall concern myself with the more intellectually challenging of the radical views of the curriculum rather than with those who would in essence abolish the curriculum in any currently recognizable form (the de-schoolers for instance); Dr Barrow, in any case, has dealt with the latter very efficiently in his *Radical Education* (1978) and I would not need to repeat his admirable work of demolition. But there are those who make out a case against the current curriculum on political grounds, alleging that it constitutes a way of preserving the current class structure, constitutes a means of control — to put it in the popular language of the *Times Educational Supplement,* a means of keeping the poor in their place. And one radical theoretician, Paulo Freire, has an interesting view of an active consciousness that can be utilized in a less revolutionary context.

II

It was about ten years ago that certain sociologists of education turned their attention from current sociological preoccupations with questions of class and social mobility to matters concerned with the content of education and knowledge. Conceptions of 'the scientific' and 'the rational', hitherto accepted unquestioningly as legitimizing categories for curriculum content, came under sociological scrutiny. It was contended that subjects or disciplines were 'socially constructed as sets of shared meanings' rather than valid absolutely

63

and as such they became proper objects of sociological enquiry. Sociologists were to treat 'what is taught, whether it be as subjects, forms of enquiry, topics, or ways of knowing' as being as problematical as traditionally anthropologists had found the belief systems of non-industrialized societies. So 'what we know' was to be regarded as an 'object of enquiry rather than a given'. (Young, 1971, pp. 9-11).

Implicit in the whole undertaking, however (an undertaking that often produces material of some interest, as in the papers of Pierre Bourdieu), there lies a value issue; and the whole sociological exercise slips from being an impartial examination of the sociological role of knowledge in educational institutions to implying an attack on the dominant thought-modes of the school system: hints of this can be found in the exposition given above. It becomes explicit in this statement by Dr M. F. D. Young:

> Formal education is based on the assumption that thought systems organized in curricula are in some sense 'superior' to the thought systems of those who are to be (or have not been) educated. It is just this implicit 'superiority' that Horton is questioning when he compares Western and African 'theoretical' thought. [1971, p. 13]

It is fair enough to treat academic culture as in some way ' "strange" and therefore "to be explained" ' (pp. 11-12); it is illegitimate to slip from such an undertaking into a pre-emptive value judgement concerning the validity of the knowledge under investigation. Thus 'an absolutist conception of a set of distinct forms of knowledge', to be found in the work of certain philosophers of education, is criticized on the grounds that these disciplines constitute '*no more than* the socio-historical constructs of a particular time' (p. 23; my italics). The useful reminder — which, of course, is completely unoriginal, for it goes back at least to the time of Bacon's analysis of the Idols of the Mind — that men *in some degree* distort the world in accordance with their pre-suppositions, interests, etc., might have legitimately stimulated a sociological investigation into the social forces at work inducing various types of distortion. This is particularly possible in the sort of 'open' society, identified by Dr Horton (1971) in the paper to which Young refers, a paper that characterizes our current scientifically oriented culture as one peculiarly willing to reconstruct views in accordance with new evidence and new experience. There are opportunities, in such a culture, for urging that class interests, personal commitments, selective viewpoints intended to preserve the *status quo* on occasions interfere with the acceptance of new insights, though only if these insights can in some way be shown to be superior to the old ones — by better fitting the 'facts', for instance — would this be necessarily reprehensible. Resistances to revised encodements could then reasonably be attributed to pre-emptive social commitments of one sort or another rather than to the state of current knowledge about the world.

But Young and his companions appear to identify such social commitments and status considerations as the only currently legitimizing factors in educational knowledge: if this were the case they would themselves be open to the same accusations that they foster against others and their own theories of legitimization would be subject to just the same charges of social and political bias as they direct against, for instance, the philosophers. In other words, the view that academic knowledge was *no more than* a socio-historical construct would necessarily itself be shown to be *no more than* a socio-historical construct. This would be both to sacrifice the element of truth in their diagnosis — 'knowledge' may well be subject on occasions to distorting factors — and yet necessarily to administer a well-earned rebuke by pointing out that sociologists themselves cannot claim immunity from the charge of perpetuating 'sociological inventions', which is the imputation made against 'academic curricula and the forms of assessment' in the last sentence of Dr Young's paper 'Curricula as socially organised knowledge' (1971, p. 41). Academic curricula may have developed in the way they have, sometimes at least, for social reasons; but society, it is as well to remind ourselves, exists in nature and has itself evolved out of its attempts to grapple with things-as-they-are. The point of identifying curricula as '*no more than* social constructs' is to undermine any element of validity such curricula might claim on the grounds that socially distorting factors — in this case the class struggle and consequent class bias — are totally disenabling; whereas behind the various social forms that have evolved with time has lain the necessity in some degree at least to conform to the world-as-it-is. A *distorted* image of the world is still an image *of the world.*

One therefore needs to ask why Dr Young and his associates have sought to push a useful reminder to an untenable degree: why do they seek to ignore the legitimizing factor of 'the world' in human knowledge and see such a legitimizing factor as constituted conventionally *only* by the power strivings of selected social groups?

The suspicion arises that they wish to play the game they impute to others; by questioning the legitimacy of the traditional curriculum, for instance, as in Dr Young's attack on the philosophers, they wish to open the way for their own legitimization of alternative curricula.

One such attempt is initiated by Miss Nell Keddie. She explicitly welcomes the lead given by the 'new sociologists' in 'casting as problematic what are held to be knowledge and ability in schools rather than taking either as given' (1971, p. 133). In further elaboration of her approval Miss Keddie contrasts the ways in which knowledge for transmission is differentiated to serve and supply the supposed 'needs' of bright and 'dull' pupils. Such descriptive terms she considers to be conventionally legitimated by the degree to which pupils fulfil teacher expectations; thus what is considered appropriate knowledge for the two groups is structured in terms of teacher expectations where bright children are concerned and at a much more 'common sense' level for the putatively dull. 'Bright' children 'are usually willing to work within the framework outlined by the teacher and within his terms' (p. 152), to the detriment of their 'autonomy'; the putatively 'dull' ones demonstrate a 'scepticism . . . which leads them to question the teachers' mode of organizing their material' (p. 151), and instead ask 'common sense' questions that could open up alternative though relevant structures. Subtly, the achievement of 'able' children is undermined and that of the 'dull' enhanced; here she exploits current approval of a critical approach to learning on the part of pupils:

> There is between teachers and 'A' pupils a reciprocity of perspective which allows teachers to define, unchallenged by 'A' pupils, as they may be challenged by 'C' pupils, the nature and boundaries of what is to count as knowledge. It would seem to be *the failure of high-ability pupils* to question what they are taught in schools that contributes in large measure to their educational achievement. [pp. 155-6; my italics]

And, indeed, an alternative principle of curriculum organization — alternative, that is, to the normal 'academic', subject-based framework — is in process of gestation: that of 'common sense' or 'ordinary experience', largely defined as the experience a child brings with him to school and therefore, in the context of the work under review, not easily distinguishable from working-class culture. This move takes place in a collection of essays edited by Miss Keddie: *Tinker, Tailor . . .* (1973). Its subtitle indicates its major purpose: 'The myth of cultural deprivation'. In her Introduction, Miss Keddie reinforces her view, implied above, that notions of 'educability' are socially constructed, in the sense that they are held to signify an ability to absorb 'mainstream' (i.e. 'middle-class') culture, whereas in fact many pupils 'are already experienced participants in a way of life', albeit one different from that which the school offers them (p. 11). There would appear to be some hesitation as to whether these alternative ways of life offer alternative educational opportunities, for both Miss Keddie and William Labov, whose study 'The logic of nonstandard English' constitutes a major contribution to the collection of essays, seem anxious at once to protect the autonomy and validity of alternative cultures and at the same time urge their possession of suitable linguistic structures for the perpetuation of those modes of abstract thinking characterizing the traditional 'middle-class' curriculum. Thus Miss Keddie argues that 'All "cultures" — class and ethnic — may have their own logics which are capable of grappling with what we shall for the moment continue to call abstract thought' (p. 18). One notes here a desire to protect the languages of groups traditionally regarded as inferior — the working classes, Negroes — from any charge that they constitute 'deprived' languages.

III

The aim, indeed, seems to be, as with black non-standard English, to foster the notion that working-class speech is a 'dialectical variation of standard English rather than a different kind of speech from that required for formal and logical thinking'; and Labov's essay seems to be much concerned to demonstrate that black non-standard dialects 'are highly structured systems' and to repudiate the notion that 'the speech of working-class people is merely a form of emotional expression, incapable of expressing logical thought' (1973, p. 61). The implication, then, may be that working-class cultures linguistically do not constitute 'deprived' forms but offer alternative ways of achieving those traditional goals of abstract thinking which are implicit in the conventional school disciplines. But it is a short step from such an imputation to the proclamation of

the autonomy of alternative cultures and life experiences — clearly
protected from any suggestion of inferiority — and to making them
the centre of educational attention. Such a step is certainly taken in
Neil Postman's essay on 'The politics of reading', which constitutes
an attack on the traditional culture of literacy by identifying it as a
means of keeping 'non-conforming youth — blacks, the politically
disaffected and the economically disadvantaged, among others —
in their place' (1973, p. 93), and recommending a new curriculum
based on the new electric media, which would enable pupils 'to
achieve what has been called 'mass-media literacy'. 'Such a school
would obviously be problem-centred, *and* future-centred, *and*
change-centred, and, as such, would be an instrument of cultural
and political radicalism' (p. 94).

Others, furthermore, are concerned to build on the traditional
features of working-class culture rather than on the new mass
media one. There is, as Mr Brian Jackson, in defending working-
class life, is partly correct in thinking '. . . some awakening sense
that mainstream working-class life is a culture the schools are not in
dialogue with, a style of life as valid as any other' (1976, p. 16). The
word 'valid' in this context, of course, receives its justification from
an attitude of mind of which Dewey's refusal to make discriminations of value as between various subjects, noted in the last chapter,
is symptomatic. The bankruptcy of the claim becomes apparent
when attempts are made to define more precisely what this working-
class culture consists of. Mr Colin McInnes in *The Times
Educational Supplement* (5 October 1973) found it in such activities
as horse and dog racing, bingo, variety, pop; the only areas with any
potential that he mentions are gardening and 'do-it-yourself' hobbies,
neither of which is by any means exclusive to the working classes.
Mr Jackson demonstrates a fitting enthusiasm for brass bands
and pigeon fancying: but he finds educational potential in chalk-
ing on walls or 'dolling up each other's hair' (1976, pp. 18-19).
Mr Chris Searle in *This New Season* finds working-class speech
superior and enjoins 'the teacher of English [to] stand up and affirm
working-class loyalties by the language that his students speak'
(1973, p. 136). The cultural inadequacy of such suggestions should
require little further comment.

Indeed, it is only possible to pretend that the working classes
today have a culture if one juggles with the meaning of the word
'culture'. Clearly, if it is interpreted in its anthropological sense as a

way of life, the working classes can be said to have a distinctive life-style; but, in its evaluative sense, the old folk culture has been destroyed by industrialization, and there are no longer elements in working-class life as such that could require the sort of structured approach implicit in the notion of schooling. As Professor Martha Vicinus has said, at the end of her study of *The Industrial Muse*, the impact of mass media entertainment has meant that 'in the twentieth century it is no longer possible to speak of a separate working-class literature' (1974, p. 280); the same could be said of music, whether folk or industrial.

At the end of all this one is left asking why the curriculum should be seen so exclusively as a matter of 'control'. Clearly there are implications to knowledge which can inhibit as well as release — but the analysis of sociologists would seem to concentrate exclusively on the former: 'pedagogic action' to implement cultural transmission is thought of in terms even of 'symbolic *violence*' (my italic) (cf. Bourdieu and Passeron, 1977). Knowledge is enabling as well as restrictive, and the concentration on the latter is no doubt revealing about the thought categories of sociologists. Is there perhaps a need for a sociological study of sociologists?

IV

Any notion, then, that working-class culture constitutes an alternative offering adaptable to the qualitative demands of the school can be dismissed. Yet some strange company is to be found sympathetic to Miss Keddie's plea that 'schools could become more flexible in their willingness to recognize and value the life experience that every child brings to school' (1973, p. 19). Professor Pring, for instance, while devastating the arguments of the new direction sociologists, nevertheless wishes to base the curriculum on precisely the 'common sense' experience children acquire in their out-of-school environment. Having had his carefully prepared social studies course ruined by the recalcitrance of his pupils (a recalcitrance he reports with an explicitness I am too old to emulate), he finds it necessary to modify his conventional philosophical concern with the development of mind in order to take cognizance of the particular problem posed by these fourth formers. He finds a solution through an exploitation of their common knowledge as the basis for their learning:

> My task with the fourth formers . . . was how to make them more thoughtful, imaginative, intelligent, etc. than they were before — for the very fact . . . that they were conscious beings meant that they already had thoughts, images, choices to make, problems to solve, feelings to control, affections etc. They were already engaged in some form of mental life . . . it was *that* that made them educable. [Pring, 1976, p. 8]

Unhappily, Professor Pring's examination of their mental life goes little further than this. It is an unexceptionable educational, methodological principle that one starts where the pupil is; but one needs great imagination to guess what precisely this encompasses. Not only does Professor Pring starve us of any relevant information concerning the conceptual grasp of his class vis-à-vis their social studies, but he has some very odd remarks to make on the whole question of conceptual understanding: 'The adolescent may have a range of concepts whereby events and objects are linked together differently from those of the teacher. His conceptual map is different, but one cannot say it is wrong.' Can't one? Immediately before this Professor Pring has urged that 'Even the young child, in lumping together all towered buildings as churches . . . has *a* way of conceiving the world, although it is not that of grown-ups' (p. 15). If a young child believes that all towered buildings are churches, then he is *wrong*: all towered buildings are *not* churches.

I am indeed puzzled that someone like Professor Pring could write such nonsense. Young children, adolescents, even university professors can have a conception of the meaning of concepts which is simply mistaken and which needs correction. Why this tenderness over mistaken understanding? One can only conjecture that the notion of cognitive relativism has spread further than one could expect. In its small way Professor Pring's surprising concession indicates the extent to which educationists are prepared to go in order to avoid suggestions of imposition, charges, ultimately, of foisting an alien culture on individuals from a putatively different tradition. Suggestions of 'refining', 'discriminating', of achieving greater 'adequacy' are just acceptable — suggestions of correction, of 'rightness' or 'wrongness' much less so. Even if we grant that language is flexible, there is no implication that it is totally tractable; certain denotations are simply mistaken.

The fact is that we have gone too far in an attempt, partly unconscious, to protect certain elements in the community from charges of inadequacy, vulgarity and the like. It is this attempt which has fostered the belief in alternative, equally 'valid' cultures and which has silenced an important tradition of social and cultural comment stretching from Arnold and before to the Leavises — and not much after. It is clear that the 'new direction' sociologists are concerned to emphasize the relativity of standards and to undermine, in effect, suggestions of high culture ('middle-class') superiority: high culture is identified as simply a ploy in the power game, a pawn in an attempt to preserve social hegemony — and would seem to have no other *raison d'être* than the bolstering of status. That it could arguably prove a more *valuable* way of taking the world is implicitly denied. What was once taken for granted, that sprang out of an implicit educational consensus, has now encountered that transvaluation of values implicit in new left ideology.

The aim of the left in previous times was to gain access, to promote greater equality of *opportunity* to participate in those high cultural activities that, at minimum, were seen as the gateway to important professions and, at best, were conceived of as affording satisfying life experiences for people traditionally excluded from them. The justification of this diagnosis lies in the overt conflict that has arisen between old and new left ideologists: Professor Brian Simon's journal *Forum* several years ago published a condemnation of 'new direction' sociologists by his wife (Simon, 1974); she argued that their ideology inhibits teachers in comprehensive schools because the belief is fostered that such teachers 'have no right to teach anything to working-class children as against respecting what they already have'. In this way, 'a formula for actual cultural deprivation of the working class' is provided. Thus the ideology of the old left implies support for the notion of cultural deprivation on the grounds of deprivation of access; the new left argues for alternative provision based on a new, indigenous, cultural identity.

V

The most forceful attempt to work out the implications of a new cultural identity (in this case, one heavily politicised) appears in the work of Paulo Freire within the context of the 'oppressed' peasant classes of the South American republics. Ostensibly addressing itself to the actualization of a suppressed consciousness submerged within an oppressive political regime, Freire's emphasis on 'reflective action' ('praxis') and his views on the pedagogic task implied in the identification of 'generative themes' as focal points are not without interest once the dangers implicit in his specific revolutionary advocacy are recognized.

Freire's book *Pedagogy of the Oppressed* reveals an up-dated rhetoric that draws on Deweyan interactionism and Marxist millenarianism and is couched in fashionable radical pseudo-egalitarian terms, which engenders an exposition highly persuasive to our politicized ears. Yet, behind the facade, lurks the age-old desire to actualize a potential implicit in the diagnostic descriptive account; Professor Freire is as prescriptive, as 'authoritarian', as any traditional theorist who overtly manifests a desire to 'fashion' or 'mould'. Let me justify this indictment.

The rhetoric, as I have said, is persuasive to modern socialized ears. There is talk of the need for 'love', for 'faith' in man. There would appear to be a radically different teacher-pupil relationship envisaged from that conventionally encountered — interaction in terms of an altered perspective, categorized as a 'teacher-student' and 'student-teacher' encounter, is recommended; the aim would seem to be the emollient one of blurring the conventional dominative aspect of teacher-pupil relationships. The teacher is to undertake the clarification of what is already latent in the consciousness of the 'oppressed' (itself a significant categorisation not explicitly justified) not by a conventional process of 'banking' pedagogy (i.e. a pedagogy that hands out material to be memorized, assimilated, on the basis of teacher domination) but through dialogue with the 'pupil', a problem-posing methodology that is intended to signal the readjustment of the traditional relationship:

> . . . the problem-posing educator constantly re-forms his reflections in the reflection of the students. The students — no longer docile listeners — are now critical co-investigators in dialogue with the teacher. The teacher presents the material to the students for their consideration, and re-examines his earlier considerations as the students express their own. [Freire, 1972, p. 54]

The problem-posing technique clearly looks back to Deweyan

instrumentalism: knowledge is conceived of not as something received into a spatialized consciousness — 'in' the mind — but as constituting a praxis, a tool for action leading to the '*emergence* of consciousness and *critical intervention* in reality' (cf. also 'Extension and Consciousness' in Freire, 1976). This 'emergence' is conceived of in terms of concepts such as 'liberation', 'reality', 'freedom', 'humanization', 'conscientization', which would seem entirely acceptable to liberally minded readers.

Yet there is a highly revealing termination to my penultimate quotation: 'The role of the problem-posing educator is to create, together with the students, the conditions under which knowledge at the level of *doxa* is superseded by true knowledge, at the level of the *logos*' (1972, p. 54). But how do we know when *doxa* has become *logos*? Which candidate for the title of the 'really' real is to receive the accolade and how is the decision to be arrived at?

In fact, the decision is pre-empted in the terms of the exposition and the underlying orientation it reveals. '*Logos*', the 'really' real, relates to those revised political conditions unveiled in the diagnostic analysis of the current state of 'oppression', which identifies the context within which the pedagogy is to function. The title of the book, indeed, reveals the polarities within which the educational discourse operates. The 'thematic universe' — the complex of the people's 'generative themes' (the terminology is Freire's, though self-explanatory) — is identified, as the operative context within which this pedagogy is to function, in the categorical statement: 'I consider the fundamental theme of our epoch to be that of *domination.* This implies that the objective to be achieved is *liberation,* its opposite theme' (1972, p. 75). The rhetoric relies, of course, on the automatically favourable and unfavourable impressions generated by notions of 'liberation' and 'domination' to achieve its prescriptive trick. Behind the pretence of modifying the 'teacher-student' consciousness through its interaction with the 'student-teacher', the terms of the 'really' real stand revealed as constituted by the preordained political manifestations implicit in the conditions of 'liberation'. The very vagueness of the specific programmatic content of the pedagogy — its lack of a clearly defined curriculum as too reminiscent of traditional 'banking' pedagogy — makes it all the more attractive; one can be swayed by the rhetoric without having to think too clearly what precisely is involved in the transition from 'domination' to 'liberation'; seemingly unexceptionable aims are confirmed, furthermore, in the postulates of a pedagogic relationship that would seem, by its very nature, to implement the desired outcome, and thus further disguise the covert authority implicit in any pedagogy.

Yet, occasionally, the rhetoric falters and a defined prescriptive intent peeps through. Underlying the whole exposition are, of course, two competing metaphysics of 'reality'; how does one emerge from one into the other?

> The starting-point for organising the programme content of education or political action must be the present, existential, concrete situation, reflecting the aspirations of the people. Utilising certain basic contradictions, we must pose this existential, concrete, present situation to the people as a problem which challenges them and requires a response — not just at the intellectual level, but at the level of action. [Freire, 1972, p. 68]

Comment seems to be called for. There is to be a 'content', then, and this, it would appear, is decided on prior to any consultation — it is to be focused on the 'present existential situation . . . reflecting the aspirations of the people'. Who decides what their aspirations are and how we come to know them? No sociological evidence is provided concerning these putative 'aspirations' nor, indeed, any evidence that the people have any. Such aspirations are, in fact, constituted of the prescriptions implied by the pedagogy, notwithstanding the reminder that we 'must never provide the people with programmes which have little or nothing to do with their own preoccupations, doubts, hopes and fears' (p. 68); for the people have already been identified, without their permission, as the 'oppressed' seeking 'liberation'; and this situation '*must*' be posed 'to the people as a problem which *challenges* them and *requires* a response' (my italics). From the permissive language of self-identification we move to the prescriptive intent of 'challenge' and 'require'. (Those content to be 'dominated' have in any case already been identified as 'emotionally dependent' — p. 40.) Even dialogue, after all, implies the domination of those who choose the subjects of discourse; and the initiative is clearly in the hands of the revolutionary pedagogues. Adult education is to include a 'literacy campaign and a post-illiteracy phase', so some content is clearly prescribed — the need to read and write. This would again appear unexceptionable — indeed, almost unquestionable — until one recalls that nagging affirmation of the greatest proletarian writer of the age, D. H. Lawrence, that 'the great mass of humanity should never learn to read and write, never' (1933, p. 77). I would agree with Freire on this, but Lawrence's injunction reminds us that Freire's programme implies a form of 'symbolic violence' which should not be allowed to slip through on the rhetoric of radical chic, and it remains at least challengeable by those who see the 'progress' of the masses in different terms.

The lengthy account given of a 'thematic investigation', which would seem to open up an awareness of mass consciousness, is vitiated by its explicit assumption that 'The only dimension of these values which it is hoped the men whose thematics are being investigated will come to share (*it is presumed that the investigators possess this quality*) is *a critical perception of the world, which implies a correct method of approaching reality in order to unveil it*' (Freire, 1972, p. 82; my italics). For all the proviso that 'critical perception cannot be imposed' (p. 83), we are back in the typically traditional pedagogic situation where some are appraised of 'real' reality and others have to be brought to it. None of the subsequent exposition does more than reveal a technique of presentation of what has been implicitly preordained as redolent of a 'potential' in contrast to a present 'self consciousness' (the terms are Freire's; cf. 1972, pp. 82-95).

Enough has been said, I hope, to reveal that Freire's exposition, like all educational theorizing, is essentially programmatic. What is reprehensible about it is not its inescapable prescriptive element but the attempt to disguise prescription beneath a rhetoric that fails to argue the case for its revolutionary intent. It may be that within the context of South American peasantry one would display a certain sympathy for some elements in its programme — but the advocacy is not self-evidently acceptable. The pretence of revealing what the masses 'really' want, of disclosing the 'true' elements of their consciousness, reveals a characteristic Marxist scientism — a claim to have identified the true march of consciousness as constituted by the revolutionary praxis. The pedagogy of problem-posing, of advocating 'teacher-student' modification in the light of the 'student-teacher's' contribution, merely obfuscates, in the rhetoric of traditional 'progressive' practice, the basically authoritarian aim of initiating into a predetermined 'really' real, instigating a politics of 'liberation', 'conscientization' and 'humanization', which need a much more explicit spelling out before they become acceptable or even open to consideration. We theorists are all prescribers, but it is up to us to prescribe in more precise curricular terms so that the commitments become assessable and arguable rather than disguised in a windy rhetoric that relies on tapping presumed emotional commitments. The traditional 'banking' pedagogy necessitated a clear articulation of the deposits to be made; 'problem-posing' has a ring of contemporary chic which disguises the very real need to decide who is to ask the questions and within which spheres of discourse they are to operate. The nearest Freire comes to admitting a traditional teacher role is in his concession that 'If educational programming is dialogical, the teacher-students . . . have the right to participate by including themes not previously suggested' (1972, p. 92). For the initiative, as in the post-literacy phase of the 'investigation of the generative themes', remains with the 'investigators', the 'teacher-students'; only the technique of presentation has changed and this differs little in essence from traditional 'progressive' explorations of themes ('centres of interest') initiated by pupils. Even the identification in conceptual terms of the move from 'real' to 'potential' consciousness to identify a desirable reorientation following a pedagogic completion is redolent of the traditional Aristotelian conception of 'actualizing' a 'potential' as the mark of educational progress. That the *technique,* especially with adults, makes, and has always made, reasonably good sense is not here the point; the point lies in the hidden intent I have revealed in this analysis, an intent the terms of which are revealed in an achieved 'potential' consciousness. (At the same time, exclusive reliance on the technique — which seems to be overtly contemplated in the revolutionary demands of dialogue, however it worked out in practice — would make what was acquired liable to the same sort of criticism I have directed against fragmentation in the chapter on 'progressivism'.) In these cases it is always necessary to look behind the surface exposition — here conceived to stress the dialogic relationship as a mutuality — and note the small print, the give-away phrases that reveal what is anticipated as outcome. Behind the persuasive rhetoric of 'liberalization', Freire's interest is revealed as a politically revolutionary outcome that can have no acceptable place within a western context where nothing in the lives of the people would justify such extreme measures.

VI

But, of course, these alternatives of the new left are not the only conceivable alternatives. The contribution of the new radical sociologists lies in their highlighting the problem that has persistently underlain all curriculum development plans since the implementation, in the later years of the last century, of universal schooling — the question of appropriate content for a total population of widely differing potential. One solution, already examined and found wanting, is that of a universal introduction to the forms of knowledge, even at appropriate levels; another is the radical solution of the alternative curriculum based on working-class cultural forms, to be condemned on the grounds of qualitative inadequacy. But, the very acceptance by members of the *left* of alternative strategies to common curricular provision is itself symptomatic of the deepening crisis now highlighted by comprehensivization.[1] The question of alternatives, seemingly inhibited if not precluded by selection difficulties, has now been implicitly raised not by the right but the left. That it has been my own solution for a number of years, though in terms very different from those of the left, now receives support in unexpected quarters — crisis makes strange bedfellows.

Furthermore, a Freirean strategy of seeking potential within the cultural consciousness of the pupils, with its proclaimed willingness to modify in accordance with present predispositions as revealed in 'dialogue' in the pedagogic situation, offers an opportunity for the delineation of a genuine folk education which can satisfy at a humanly symbolic level; one can employ the technique without the highly dangerous totalitarian implications that characterize Freire's revealed intent. Any alternative curriculum, indeed, must arise out of a *limited* Freirean strategy of questioning the nature of folk consciousness in its typical manifestations; it must involve, that is, an attempt at an imaginative understanding of the bounds within which folk awareness can reasonably be expected to operate, and an assessment of its congruity with the new demands made on it.[2]

NOTES

1. There is even a call by Paul Willis (1977) for 'independent *working class* educational institutions' (p. 189; my italics). This would seem to imply some

form of class 'segregation', at least for certain disaffected 'lads'. I can imagine the furore I would have aroused if *I* had made any such suggestion. One sympathises with Mr Willis' dilemma — *Learning to Labour* reveals a pretty desperate situation, though I am not sure whether Mr Willis himself would interpret it in this way.

2. I stress 'limited' because Freire himself would no doubt see implicit in my employment of his technique an element of paternalism — and to a degree he would be right. But then, despite all his protests, I find the same in him, as I hope to have made clear in my analysis of his work.

CHAPTER 5

The Alternative Curriculum

I

I shall begin with an historical, cultural analysis of the implications of the culture of literacy — and therefore of the curriculum of 'knowledge' and mind defined in the first chapter — in order to assess the nature and viability of current demands on a total population in curricular terms. For, of course, knowledge, in the modern sense, arose out of literacy — the ability to codify and preserve.

Literacy became a defining feature in the education of the ruling classes during the Renaissance, as I have indicated in the first chapter, and it was at this time that the first great educational revolution of the last thousand years took place. The crucial element in the second revolution, the revolution of the last hundred years, involves the extension of this traditionally elite literacy to the total population. I don't know of any previous civilization that has attempted this. Fifth-century Athens appears to have had a high rate of literacy but it did not extend to the total population. The Jews, too, have always been highly literate, but they did not build a nation until recently, living as a series of sub-cultures within other nations.

I should perhaps here offer a brief gloss on my phrase, 'the extension of this traditionally elite literacy to the total population'. I am aware of the fact that there is an earlier popular literature — street ballads and chap-books, for example — which points to a certain level of literacy developing among the folk from the mid-fifteenth century, when the invention of moveable type enabled a more rapid dissemination of printed material. Despite such evidence of literacy, especially during the seventeenth century, basically the culture of the folk stemmed from an oral rather than a literary tradition, and when, following the Act of 1870, the need to acquire literacy became gradually obligatory for the total population, it was a diluted elite literacy that was imposed on the new inhabitants of the schools. A glance at the work of W. R. Mullins (1968) indicates how the textbooks used at that time in the teaching of English reflected the taste, perhaps a somewhat watered-down taste, of the Victorian upper and middle classes. It comprised the typical romantic offerings spiced with rather inferior writings, such as those of Mrs Hemans. There was no hint in the new schools of traditional folk literature — printed street ballads and the like — or oral material, telling about life in pre-industrial times. This situation continued until around the turn of the century, when Cecil Sharp rediscovered and redeployed for educational uses something of the heritage of folk music and dance; but music has always been a peripheral subject.

The core of our new endeavour, then, was a new kind of culture — new, that is, to the masses — transmitted in what was for many of them a new way, a new medium. To get to the heart of our current discontent at the popular level it is therefore necessary to examine the nature of these new meanings and especially the way in which they were to be transmitted, and thus assess their potential for those stemming from a different cultural tradition.

II

Let me begin by examining the medium, on the grounds that, in some degree, the medium *is* the message (an exaggeration of a vital truth that the medium structures in ways unique to its character the particular message that is being transmitted). It is notorious that reading a political speech is often a very different matter from hearing it spoken by an orator of some power, and the difference arises not out of the content but from emotional force that discriminates the spoken from the written word. It is indeed astonishing how little we have examined the implications of the act of reading — as an occupation central to a culture, not simply as a peripheral distraction — and yet the first thing that a child does when he goes to school is to learn to read. The book is the basis of much of the superstructure of the school culture. 'Get out your books' is still the ritual that opens the majority of school lessons.

The essence of the Renaissance ideal was a fusion of the active and contemplative principles. Action, however, was to be based on knowledge, while correspondingly knowledge without action was thought of as wasted. In this amalgamation of the active and contemplative principles it was thought that the Platonic ideal would be reborn. Symbolically, we may allow the famous picture of Frederico da Montefeltre, Duke of Urbino, attributed to Pedro Berruguete, to represent the new ideal. The great duke, one of the two or three most highly cultured ruling princes of the Italian Renaissance, sits at his reading desk dressed in a suit of armour — in his role as Captain-General of the Church — with a volume open in front of him which he holds in his hands, propped up against the desk, and his little son, Guidobaldo, the ruler in Castiglione's *The Courtier,* by his side. There is no hint that reading is likely to inhibit action. The duke is at rest, poised and alert, for there is a certain tension in the pose behind the surface relaxation, which suggests that contemplation could quickly dissolve into action.

Professor Edgar Wind, too, has destroyed the vulgar notion that there is any *necessary* opposition between action of another sort — artistic action — and learning based on reading and understanding. In his Reith lectures, *Art and Anarchy,* he points out that 'It is known from historical evidence that great art has been produced . . . by artists of the highest degree of literacy. Having eaten from the Tree of Knowledge, we cannot slip backwards into paradise: the gate is locked and the angel behind us, but the garden may be open at the opposite end' (1963, p. 67). He adds that 'Anyone reading the letters of Titian, Michelangelo or Rubens, or perusing the verbal jests which it pleased Leonardo da Vinci or Mozart to invent, must be impressed . . . by their literary ease' (p. 58).

Yet pervasively throughout western thought it has been continually hinted that there is an uneasy split between action and consciousness. It is, indeed, true that language itself is a symbolic system rather than a system of signs — a means by which man can abstract from, rather than simply respond to, the external world — and thus a phenomenon that raises acute problems concerning the precise relationship between mind and world. As man is capable not only of reacting but also of reflecting on and hence controlling his reactions, he can never, as D. H. Lawrence pointed out, be spontaneous as we imagine the thrush or the sparrowhawk, for example, to be spontaneous. Yet, if the phenomenon of language is itself sufficient for the development of an 'inner' consciousness, it may well be admitted that the incidence of literacy, the ability to read and write, involves a considerable extension of this inner domain.

Let us, then, look further at these implicit demands of literacy and their effects on consciousness, and, for the sake of brevity, let us concentrate on reading.

III

I have dealt with this problem at some length in the inaugural lecture I gave at Leicester University entitled 'The Implications of Literacy' (1965). To summarize briefly, the act of reading implies a highly complex internal translation system for which the clues provided are much fewer than they are for the act of listening. Gesture, intonation, pitch, rhythm, facial expression and so on, all in some degree aid the listener. The reader has to supply all these emphases from the interpretation of immobile marks on a page of inanimate material. As R. G. Collingwood puts it, 'The written or printed book is only a series of hints from which the reader works out the hints which alone have the gift of expression' (1955, p. 243). For one thing, then, reading lacks the emotion expressed by the human vagaries of speech. It demands not only the psychological conditions necessary for efficient inner translation (which may explain why in a literate age poetry, which involves the most complex form of language and makes correspondingly greater inner demands, has become, at most, the interest of a minority), but also the social conditions of silence and apartness. If meaning is to be construed through some form of inner sense, and the marks translated with the necessary rhythms and emphases, the social conditions necessary for this functioning deserve some comment.

The library, the study, are rooms traditionally set apart from family living. The complaint 'always got his head stuck in a book' symbolizes the often resented apartness that reading implies. Around himself the reader creates a zone of social silence; physically his movements are confined to tiny regular twitchings of the eye. This means that amidst social classes where such conditions are not easily come by in terms, for instance, of room space, or where, traditionally, gregariousness is valued and apartness frowned upon, certain sections of the community's children may find themselves under both psychological and social pressure to ignore reading as a normal element in their daily lives. Also the emphasis that the school places upon the need to acquire understanding through books introduces an alien element into the sub-culture from which these children come. As a medium, then, reading raises fundamental social and cultural questions to which we have perhaps paid too little attention. As Professor L. Stone puts it,

> The conversion of childhood, which is normally and naturally a time of play and random physical activity, into one of sedentary book learning must have important effects on the adult character, producing the self-discipline and punctuality needed for a modern society, but perhaps also a severe if latent sense of frustration. [1969, p. 94]

How great must this frustration prove among sections of the population ill-prepared historically for its demands and possessing little insight into its rewards.

IV

A previous point — the link I made earlier between reading, consciousness and action — I want now to consider further in the light of that simple statement already referred to, made by a former elementary-school teacher of universally acknowledged genius: 'The great mass of humanity should never learn to read and write — never'. Let me re-emphasise straight away that I do not endorse this comment. It does, however, make us ask some quite fundamental questions about the nature of literacy and its implications for certain kinds of minds in our society. Its significance in the body of D. H. Lawrence's writings certainly is clear enough. Lawrence's work can be regarded, in part, as an extended commentary on the concept of spontaneity, or, to put it another way, he is deeply concerned with the nature of the relationship between action and consciousness. His analysis, indeed, has much in common with a similar one made by

Nietzsche in his studied objections to the appearance of what he termed 'theoretical man' — a new, yet highly significant, type of being characteristic of his own day and even more of ours. Nietzsche considered theoretical man the victim of the illusion that 'thought, guided by the thread of causation, might plumb the furthest abyss of being and even *correct* it'. Such a person, Nietzsche thought, is 'strong in the belief that nature can be fathomed, considers knowledge to be the true panacea and error to be radical evil' (1956, pp. 92-4). Thought, then, should precede and control action. Socrates, he considers, stood as the forerunner of this belief that life was consciousness and rationality rather than instinctual urge and spontaneity. And Nietzsche sees this as, in some degree, a deprivation.

Consciousness to Lawrence, of course, implied 'ideas' — the abstractions characteristic of a section of the community deeply oriented to rationalism in a society dominated, even in its structural life, by an administrative bureaucracy marked, in Max Weber's words, by 'rational matter-of-factness'. Our society is one in which, ideally, we arrive at decisions on the basis of supposed evidence rather than intuition, and is distinguished by 'the general habit of questioning, wondering, answering' (Sprott, 1967, p. 25); this has been made clear in my description of curriculum evolution given in the first chapter. In such a society, characteristically, it is constantly stressed that a major purpose of the educational system is to make children 'critical' of their environment. Such a society also thinks that all problems are susceptible to elucidation and solution — preferably by a committee — and the word 'problem' has itself become one of the major concepts of the twentieth century.

My theme in this chapter, then, is the extension of consciousness and awareness implicit in this phenomenon of literacy with its accompanying emphasis on rationality and abstract thought, and its relevance to a section of the population traditionally oriented to direct action — the action of comparatively unreflective speech, of immediate practicality unalloyed by theory, the action of those whose work habits are acquired by contact and copying, whose songs and expressive life spring out of a manifestation, as Willa Muir puts it in her *Living with Ballads,* of 'energies not concepts' (1965, p. 33). Today, even a university student may be found saying 'I know what I think when I do something about it' — a fascinating statement of the tendency of many students, even some of the more sophisticated ones, to define themselves in terms of action rather than reflection. Furthermore, Freire's experience with the traditionally uneducated revealingly leads him to emphasize a close relationship between reflection and action as the outcome of his recommended pedagogy.

It is interesting fo note, indeed, that traditionally the phenomenon of reading and the learning that accompanied it aroused suspicion and apprehension. Early in the Middle Ages a group of Goths told Queen Amalasuntha that 'Letters are removed from manliness and the teaching of old men results for the most part in a cowardly and submissive spirit' (Cipolla, 1969, p. 41) — a remark worth quoting because it curiously echoes D. H. Lawrence's statement that many people in the working classes of his time thought reading and learning constituted a sort of 'unmanliness'. The reason was that thought, and the consciousness that accompanied it, was considered to inhibit activity, human responsiveness.

Lawrence's message is that reasoned awareness is contrary to the nature of his folk who behave, to revert to Willa Muir's phrase, in response to 'energies not concepts'; such reasoning as they do most easily exercise arises out of concrete actualities rather than the abstractions of social and political life. While I believe, then, that there is no reversion from the current commitment to more consciousness, a process by which what was formerly intuitive, imitative or habitual gradually becomes increasingly subject to reasoned assessment and conscious deliberation — a process that it is the ultimate function of the school to further — I also believe that for certain sections of the school population its implementation needs to be a slow and deliberate one. We should, indeed, bring into question the specific contexts within which it is reasonable to expect low achieving children to exercise judgement or to express themselves in abstract terms. The progressive technique, adopted by Freire, of initiating a pedagogy in theory at least intended to relate to the actualities of folk consciousness, has an important role to play in the assessment of possibilities.

V

Here, then, we begin to approach the problem of the current low achiever. Perhaps I ought to begin by making it clear that this problem is not susceptible to a single approach, for low achievement is a complex manifestation. It may, for instance, betoken emotional disturbance among children of reasonably high intelligence; it may spring from undetected physical disabilities such as poor sight or hearing. But not all failure can be explained in this way. The children I have specifically in mind are those perhaps most clearly defined in the pages of the Schools Council inquiry, *Young School Leavers*, and I quote from the introduction to that inquiry:

> . . . those affected will have an aptitude for scholastic work which is average or below average. Some will come from homes which attach small value to extended schooling. For many vocational motivation will be weak; it will be difficult to engage their interest and sense of relevance. Some will actively resent having to stay longer in school. [1968, p. iii]

I would be happy if, in the first place, the suggestions I shall make later could be applied to approximately the bottom 25 per cent of the age group and throughout their secondary school careers. They will be children of low achievement and probably, though not invariably, of low IQ. They will come from culturally deprived homes (in the sense certainly that it will be a home without books), wish to leave school as soon as possible, and on leaving find themselves employed in unskilled or semi-skilled jobs.

With these children I believe the core of the problem lies in the conflict between their socio-cultural potential and the implicit demands of the school culture, for that culture, as previously indicated, has become primarily cognitive in orientation, demanding an extended consciousness that accords ill with the traditional unreflectiveness of the folk, its orientation towards action.

If we take the Freudian model of human behaviour we may see the development of the rational ego as the somewhat reluctant outgrowth of the basic instinctual drives, and if we take Piaget's model we find that a considerable section of the school population will probably remain at the stage of concrete operations rather than develop into formal operations. And indeed, Dr Hallam's research into children's capacity to grasp historical concepts concludes that 'the majority of secondary school pupils up to a mental age of 16 years seem to be at the concrete operational level of thought' (1969a, p. 3). All this confirms Nietzsche's view that

Consciousness is the last and latest development of the organic, and is consequently the most unfinished and least powerful of these developments. Every extension of knowledge arises from making conscious the unconscious; the great basic activity is unconscious. For it is *narrow*, this room of human consciousness. [1956]

Traditionally, as I have pointed out, the folk consciousness has been one of practicality and emotionality, finding its outlet in folk art and imitative skills rather than abstract thought, in particulars rather than universals. Throughout much of European history, indeed, we find the same story. Thus medieval preachers exhibited a desire 'to escape as far as possible from the abstract and universal in religion, and to be "at home in particulars" ' (Owst, 1933, p. 110). Folk culture in general depended on 'a stock of forms (schemata, motifs, themes, formulae)' that betrays a dependence on the stereotyped and the traditional (Burke, 1978, p. 124). In the nineteenth century, George Bourne identified 'the subjects of the moment — that endless procession of things seen or heard' as the area within which it was easiest to make contact with the peasant mind; such a mind had no 'habit of interpreting these phenomena by general ideas or abstract principles' (1920, pp. 195-6). This remains characteristic of their speech. Professor Bernstein, indeed, has defined their restricted speech code as 'particularistic': it is 'context bound', that is, 'tied to local relationships and to local social structure' unlike that of the more conscious classes. Such codes 'draw upon metaphor whereas elaborated codes draw upon rationality' (1971, p. 176). Furthermore, present-day industrial relations contain numerous instances where myth rather than complex rational analysis dominates the workers' assessment of a situation. In an interesting article called 'Myth and attitude change', A.J.M. Sykes speaks of the role of myth in the workshop. In his study 'The case of the brutal foremen' he shows how in a particular factory strong attitudes of hostility towards foremen arose out of a stereotype of the foreman based largely on past history:

> by the early 1950s all the more brutal foremen had retired and been replaced by more reasonable men. However, the stereotype of the foreman remained unaltered because the conditions which had led to its creation — the brutality of past foremen — were kept alive by oral tradition in the works. [1965, p. 329]

Dr Sykes provides a fascinating analysis of the basic patterns that this story and others like it followed. In general, the attitude to foremen was changed by constructing counter-myths rather than through rational assessment and argument. Such a continuity of evidence, from the medieval pulpit to the modern factory, though necessarily only briefly evocative in a small book, is nevertheless highly impressive.

In the work life of the people, then, we may note emotional, dramatic, artistic elements as characteristic of their preference for taking life 'instinctively and intuitively', as D.H. Lawrence puts it. Similar evidence of the importance of emotional appeal can be gleaned, of course, from the mass media and especially from advertising, which appeals in terms of images and emotional content rather than attempts at rational persuasion. All around us, indeed, is evidence supporting the belief that learning, for considerable sections of the population, must operate at an emotional, mythical, imagistic level. Only educationists fail to learn the lesson.

VI

It might seem then that our questioning has raised doubts about the viability of current commitments and at the same time provided some of the clues for a revised approach. There are, in the first place, the specifically social pressures that make schooling unpalatable, for example its appearance of unmanliness. Then there is the emphasis on rationality, the implication of long-term objectives unpalatable to a section of the community used to seeking immediate satisfaction (in itself an indication of the preference for action over rationality), and the demand for a level of conceptual development beyond the grasp of many in terms of their characteristic speech patterns. All point to a fundamental cleavage in terms of behaviour — the conflict of action and consciousness — between the home sub-culture and the school. Clearly, it is reasonable to anticipate that our cognitively oriented curriculum is likely to prove inappropriate for minds that function at a more concrete and emotional level. How, then, do we go about seeking an alternative?

It is not without significance that the arts, apart from literature, which comes later anyway, depend on articulation through gestures

— dance, drama, painting, sculpture and crafts of many kinds — and that their initial orientation is towards a celebration of the community. It is as though man's more primitive way of taking in his world is through the discipline of movement and the physical exploration of space that it allows him.

If reading is the gateway to the world of inner consciousness, then some form of action through movement education may well be the key to authentic emotional experience. By expressing ideas in concrete form and in their most primitive manifestation of dance, it affords opportunities for communal participation, and may tie in with what we know of the potentialities of the generally less intellectually endowed reluctant learners. (I use movement education in the sense most fully developed and defined in the work of Rudolf Laban.) D.H. Lawrence found the centre of the dynamic self to be in the region of the solar plexus. Interestingly enough, exponents of modern dance insist on the centring of dance movement in the torso rather than the head — at the centre of emotion rather than of consciousness, that is. There is already interesting evidence in England of the educative benefits that some kinds of dramatic play and movement can bestow on subnormal children. In an article entitled 'The theatre of the subnormal', Miss Patience Tuckwell writes of severely subnormal children:

> As a source of development the child's imagination has been relatively untapped. Previous research done in large sub-normality hospitals seems to have misled researchers into believing that there was a lack of will — indeed a lack of imagination among patients. It now seems to have been a lack of experience and stimulation that led patients to accept whatever was required of them as inevitable.[1971]

As far as the children Patience Tuckwell herself was teaching were concerned, during their earlier years many valuable things had been done for them. There had been ample provision for the exploration of plastic media, sounds and textures, and a sense of drama had been included.

> I set out to use this to its utmost limits. Dramatic play is not just the playing out of anxiety-ridden experiences — though doubtless this needs to be done — it is the reconstruction of many experiences that the child is having daily — the construction of abstract ideas in a tangible form, and fathoming and remaking of the world, the extension of the personality.

After describing in detail some of the specific devices used — dance, mime, drama and painting — she concludes that the time allowed for this work was too brief in view of the children's retarded development and that the children left too soon. 'Given an extended period of liberal education they might be expected to find in themselves the qualities they seem so often to lack — poise, self-confidence, purpose, initiative and practical ambitions.'

The world of the mongol can be regarded as an intensified form of the world of dullness to which many of the children about whom we are here concerned may be said to belong. T.R. Fyvel (1960) discovered that even his 'insecure offenders' would respond to the rhythms and invitation to movement implicit in modern pop music.[1] The Greeks noted an analogous response to musical stimuli. Not a noticeably unintellectual people, they realized that the ultimate roots of conduct are emotional. 'Nothing', as Plato said in *The Laws*, 'is so native to men as pleasure, pain, and desire. They are, so to say, the very wires or strings from which any mortal nature is inevitably and absolutely dependent' (V, 732), and Plato realized the educational significance of this: 'No young creature whatsoever . . . can keep its body or its voice still; all are perpetually trying to make movements and noises. They leap and bound, they dance and frolic, as it were with glee, and again, they utter cries of all sorts' (II, 653).

The principle, then, is that of movement and activity — activity, however, in a different sense from that of conventional progressive parlance. There it implies a methodological device, a harnessing for motivational reasons of the children's natural energy resources for direct initiation into intellectual matters. Here I use it to mean the kinetic basis of the curriculum I am advising. The discipline will be that of posture and movement seeking a variety of significant forms. It implies attention to the emotions because it takes normally random impulses of children and directs them into ordered activities. In this way emotions may be expressed in orderly and patterned activity in the creation, in Professor Susanne Langer's terms, of a world both reflecting and in some degree different from the real world. At the same time the ultimate aim involves an approach to consciousness; for it is a fundamental error not to see that, as the arts develop, they inevitably come to involve knowledge and understanding — a point made clear earlier by my reference to Professor Wind's *Art and Anarchy*.

VII

I must now give some particulars of what I would advocate in this emphasis on expressive action as the key to emotional discipline. As I have indicated, the sort of movement education I have in mind as a basis is that which Rudolf Laban has done so much to develop and which is being used to some extent in the education of children in England, especially at the primary level. This type of movement education involves a disciplined exploration of space involving the expression of inner feelings, and the images of human behaviour they evoke. At the same time Laban indicates that 'Dance is not to relieve feelings, it is not self-expression; dance is no longer spontaneous gestures but deliberate acts' (quoted in Bruce, 1965, p. 33), *for all arts involve a making and not simply an outlet.* It is this that makes them educative rather than therapeutic. This type of movement merges into dance as a socialized participatory form, becoming an art form, an articulation of gestures, and offering opportunities for thought in construction, thought, however, geared to the actualities of conduct and derived from the observation of behaviour.

Anyone who has had any experience of dance movement will have a broad view of what I have in mind. Laban-inspired dance education implies the possibility of achieving forms of aesthetic expression through bodily movement. In the process of creation, children are asked to think about how they can deploy the language of movement they have acquired in ways that communicate their understanding of aspects of the real world in articulated though non-linguistic form. Stimuli in the real world may provide a narrative framework or simply an initial impulse towards expression. But in the process what is achieved becomes manifest not as a mindless set of random impulses but as an ordered succession of gestures and movements conveying their appreciation both of states of mind and of their awareness of acceptable and recognizable ways of representing those states of mind to others. 'Dance' thus mingles both personal and public elements; and it is this orientation towards a publicly acceptable expressiveness which implies an observation of the real world and a developing consciousness as to the ways in which such expressiveness can be made meaningful to others. It provides a medium, for instance, through which the linguistic forms of narrative or poetry can be translated into physically expressive terms, and thus enable children who are linguistically limited to come to some apprehension of what is intended; or it may involve absorbing the rhythms and mood of music and redeploying them in a personalised, expressive, publicly recognizable manner. Movement education, indeed, provides an alternative way of coming to terms with other public modes of utterance in ways more specific and concrete than merely through intellectual assimilation. 'Understanding' can be promoted through the search for appropriate gesture; it expresses in kinetic terms what might well prove, for less verbally articulate children, difficult to verbalize adequately.

And, indeed, there are important links with other art forms — literature, music, mime and drama. Once we move into the world of drama we are involved in the symbolic system of language, in this case oral language. Here we should pay much more attention than we do to what Professor Andrew Wilkinson of the University of Exeter has called 'oracy', the ability to speak and converse. Children should learn how to build up oral discourse in a variety of modes, expository, explanatory, narrative, etc.

At the same time, reading and writing must inevitably form an important, indeed essential, part of the work but they will arise out of the activities rather than form the central core of these children's culture. Other aspects of disciplined movement merge into design and craft work and art in two or three dimensions. A Schools Council Project under the direction of Professor Eggleston, the advisory body of which I was myself the chairman, has, I think, shown the way forward into areas of significance where traditional craft work is linked with a profounder awareness of design and the need to involve the children in the matter of planning and choice.

The other area that should form part of the school curriculum for these children arises out of the characteristic twentieth-century art forms — film, television, radio. Film making and editing, and photography, are means through which children can develop iconographic awareness, which is part of the twentieth-century cultural consciousness. This heightened consciousness, then, helps the child to benefit from the use of television, the 'major' medium of communication in our age.

I must make it clear that what I have in mind here is an attempt to improve the quality of children's responses to the media — not simply a technical understanding of how what they hear or see has been put together and transmitted, though, of course, the realization of the technical potentialities of the medium will inevitably play an important part in appreciation. It is necessary to face the implications of a popular culture that transmits expressive material inadequate to the quality and complexity of the emotional life of its viewers, a culture not only inadequate, but perhaps positively harmful. As Professor Susanne Langer has put it,

> People who are so concerned for their children's scientific enlightenment that they keep Grimm out of the library and Santa Claus out of the chimney, allow the cheapest art, the worst of bad singing, the most revolting sentimental fiction to impinge on the children's minds all day and every day, from infancy. If the rank and file of youth grows up in emotional cowardice and confusion, sociologists look to economic conditions or family relations for the cause of this deplorable 'human weakness', but not to the ubiquitous influence of corrupt art, which steeps the average mind in a shallow sentimentalism that ruins what germs of true feeling might have developed in it. [1953, pp. 401-2]

It is sometimes argued that this sort of material has no effect on us, which is tantamount to saying that what we see, read or listen to is without consequence, a proposition I would have thought distressing to any teacher. That social scientists find the *precise* effects hard to measure is not necessarily an indication that there are none, for they are unlikely to be of the dramatic nature that leads to direct and overt social consequences. As Richard Hoggart put it, 'You cannot demonstrate emotional debility' (quoted in Halloran, 1964, p. 40). What occurs — one's own experience bears this out — is a slow erosion of one's finer potentialities under the incessant influence of cheap stereotypes of human conduct and simplistic images of human behaviour. My own experience — I was of the first generation to grow up in a media world — is that of being surrounded by an all-pervasive miasma of false views and images that one had to battle one's way through in order to achieve any understanding of the reality of human relationships and the human situation. Previous civilizations have succumbed to barbarian invasions from outside; our enemy lurks in the corner of our sitting room, ready to perform his corrosive function at the turn of a knob.

Of course, the media offer immense opportunities as well as threats. It is the use to which they are put that matters. In improving the response to the media, one is aiding the education of the emotions that the age of Freud would see as a fundamental desideratum of any educational system. Clearly the school can only contribute in a limited way to emotional growth; it is not a therapeutic institution. But by placing in front of children forms expressive of emotional refinement and complexity and by introducing them to a range of emotionally oriented material suggestive of half-forgotten positive feelings such as those of grace, decorum, harmony and nobility, teachers may play a larger part in offsetting what L.H. Myers termed the 'deep-seated spiritual vulgarity which lies at the heart of our civilisation' (1935, pp. 10-11). Poetry, music, good cinema and television provide opportunities for emotional involvement in expressive forms that can feed rather than destroy the finer responses. Of this I shall have more to say at the end of this chapter.

In addition to the suggestions for a curriculum already made, there should also be some emphasis on the physical life — games, the opportunities that form part of the new physical education. All this should take up about three fifths of the children's time. For the rest there should be an emphasis on domestic life primarily for girls but that boys should be encouraged to share, and aspects of technical education for boys but also for girls to a greater extent than at present. In this way, understanding can be built up in relation to concrete decision making; cognition grows out of the practical disciplines of social and technical life. Also this will enable some of our industrial needs to be met — needs that it would be irresponsible to ignore. (At the same time, contrary to the conventional wisdom in these matters, I think our purely technical education is in a more satisfactory state than our current artistic and humanistic culture, which is threatened by debasing and trivializing forces that would have no place in the technical field.)

VIII

Anyone who attempts to meet the problem of the low achiever by framing an alternative curriculum, not as a few additional suggestions but as a radical reorientation of principle, even if it uses elements already to be found in some schools, must be prepared to meet certain criticisms. The criticisms my suggestions have provoked can be roughly categorized into three groups — philosophical, social and political, and what might be broadly termed practical. Clearly, to some extent the categories overlap, but some such sorting out enables me to concentrate on answering points in an orderly manner.

The more technical, philosophical objections can be dealt with quite rapidly as in most cases they stem from an insufficiently exact reading of what I have had to say. Thus I have been accused of holding an expressionist theory of art, a charge against which my quotation from Laban, with its rejection of dance as the relief of feelings and its emphasis on 'deliberate acts', dance essentially as a shaping and a making, should have protected me. I see these activities as disciplines, not simply as out-pourings or releases; I am concerned with education, not therapy. Then, astonishingly, I am accused of perpetuating an affective/cognitive dichotomy, as if I believed that disciplines could be allocated exclusively to one or the other category. I have made it abundantly clear in a number of places that I accept no such dichotomy (e.g. 1967, Chap. 3, 'The education of the emotions'; 1968, pp. 73-81); and, indeed, I have stated specifically that my 'ultimate aim' constitutes an 'approach to consciousness and mind (. . . it is a fundamental error not to see that, as the arts develop, they inevitably come to involve knowledge and understanding)'; it could hardly be more explicit. It is really not possible, every time I refer to the 'emotional' disciplines, to add 'with their cognitive implications' — though that, let the reader be assured, is what is intended.

A more interesting point, and one of more general interest, urges that it is a mistake to think that less able children will necessarily find the disciplines of movement less exacting than disciplines of other kinds:

> . . . the discipline of *composing*, of wrestling with motifs, contrasts . . . is just as rigorous and demanding in dance . . . as in any other art. And the ability of intellectually less able children . . . to imagine, to formulate and to structure, is hardly likely to be less limited than in other fields. [Redfern, 1975, p. 40]

Of course, such children will produce work in the various arts and crafts that is likely to be of limited value, and I see no reason to doubt that intellectually able children will, in general, shine also in artistic subjects. But the important point is that intellectually limited children can, in general, make some sort of a shot at the affectively oriented subjects whereas they are totally lost, in the majority of cases, where the more cognitively oriented subjects are concerned. We all have bodies, though some are inevitably clumsier in their movements than others; the ungainly will produce less refined results than their more graceful compeers. But comparable cognitive demands will produce no results whatsoever from the intellectually dull.

Some, of course, would deny this last point and urge that a denial of common cognitive opportunities to all children cannot be justified, on the grounds that the potential of such children can never be gauged with sufficient accuracy to justify their allocation, at a comparatively early age, to an alternative educational diet. We now begin to become involved in arguments with social and political overtones.

Are there, then, rational grounds for believing that some children are constitutionally incapable of following an intellectually demanding curriculum? We have already encountered Mr White's view in Chapter 3 that such a view is 'not a rational belief, it is rather an article of faith', and the time has come to make good my promise to adduce rational grounds for supporting my position.

Let me first repeat my admission that such a contention of incapacity could not be *proved;* indeed, to expect proof would be irrational, for it is clearly not reasonable to expect man to do what by nature he is incapable of doing, that is to predict, infallibly, the future. It is only reasonable to expect men to proceed on grounds that can be defended rationally as appertaining to the nature of the case in hand.

Now, when a child enters a secondary school of any type, comprehensive or other, inevitably a decision has to be taken as to what he is to learn there. The fact that in many comprehensive schools this question is not formally asked — because it is the set policy of the school that all children shall follow a common curriculum — does not mean that a decision has not in fact been taken. (There is somehow a belief that *not* to allocate children to different learning programmes obviates the need for justification. But not to allocate involves just as much of a decision requiring justification as does allocation. *All* educational decisions concerning curricular choices involve value judgements and need therefore to be capable of rational justification. The fact that the decision is allowed to go by default is simply indicative of our current social idiosyncracies.)

It is idiotic to argue that there is no evidence available to help those who would be responsible for allocating children to the sort of curriculum I am suggesting. There are reports from the primary schools, the results of intelligence and achievement tests, knowledge about home background and parental support, opportunities for close consultation with previous teachers. After all, any child of secondary school age has already undergone a five-year period during which diagnosis can be carried out; one could only wish that all our social decisions could be taken with such a weight of evidence available.

I have already admitted that such evidence can never be totally definitive, and would freely grant that occasional errors will almost inevitably be made. But this is always true of any academic or social decision that is ever made. Human beings are not gods, and they must, as I have urged, learn to operate within the restrictions that the fallibility of human capacity for prediction necessarily imposes.[2] In the light of the sort of evidence I have listed above, it is perfectly reasonable to predict that some children, at least, will be unable to cope with an intellectually demanding curriculum. We are not proceeding irrationally or on the basis of what our critic intends to imply by 'faith'; we are proceeding responsibly, on the basis of the best evidence available. Indeed, it would be perfectly reasonable to throw the onus of decision-making onto Mr White by asking him on what grounds, in the face of the available evidence, he would argue that certain specific children show any potential whatsoever for the sort of curriculum he has in mind. As the husband of someone who has taught remedial reading in a state primary school for many years I would be delighted to attend and listen to discussions about the potential of specific children in the light of experience of such children gathered over a long period of time. I know, too, that my wife would readily welcome those suggestions for alternative methods that in the eyes of our critic would appear to offer the promise of turning her geese into swans.

'Ah! that's it', I can hear other critics exclaim — 'geese' and 'swans'; I am labelling some children as inferior. Actually, geese, to anyone who has looked at them properly, are fine, handsome birds; and swans can be ill-natured beasts. But it so happens that, however much one may wish nature had arranged things differently, geese just aren't swans. There is an indication of this sort of criticism in the accusation that my aim is simply to keep "the folk" happy at their own level' (cf. Simon, 1974, p. 13). There is not, I think, anything inherently wicked in the attempt to make people happy; but, in fact, the implications behind the accusation should not be allowed to stand. Indeed, one very important consideration that reconciles me to the likelihood of error in some degree at least in the matter of allocation arises from the nature of the alternative curriculum I am offering. It seems to me to afford two sorts of opportunity. There are, in the first place, possible occupational opportunities. One of the major practical objections that has been urged against my scheme is that by adopting it we shall be spoiling the occupational opportunities of the children concerned, cutting them off from the sort of prestige job that requires a type of certification geared to the conventional curriculum.

But what in fact at present faces the sort of child I have defined here? Not indeed a prestige job but repetitive work in a factory of the soul-destroying type that constitutes one of the great dilemmas of our technological civilization. On the other hand, what I would offer them certainly has its occupational possibilities. The increase in leisure — likely to be exacerbated in the age of the silicon chip — and the proliferation of popular art forms that the revolution in communications of our times has led to is engendering new occupations of various types. Characteristic of these new occupations are the emotional features that it is the job of my curriculum to afford some training in — and some protection against the vulgarity (and worse) fostered by these manifestations is in any case sorely needed. If we offer the sort of curriculum I am suggesting to our low achievers, it is perfectly reasonable to hope that some, at least, will mature in a way the present cognitive emphasis of the curriculum has signally failed to assist. In other words, I am suggesting that opportunities will be afforded — in the sphere of communications, for instance — which at present do not exist for these children. I am not so romantic as to think that all or even many will be able to seize these opportunities; but they certainly will not be — they could not be — worse off than they are at the moment.

Then there are other opportunities that stem from the quality of the material itself. This is not one of those life-adjustment programmes with its exclusive emphasis on the banalities of daily life (I shall say more about these in a moment); it is not an education for helots. To be acceptable to the conscience of the age it must contain a strong element that is genuinely liberalizing — and this is precisely what it does. It can open up many of the riches of

European civilization, for it exploits, for instance, a number of the same devices that the medieval church employed in its attempt to transmit its message to the people. (It is interesting to note that many of these popular devices — the paintings, the sculptures, the music, etc. — have gradually down the ages become the preserves of the elite. Why? A good remedial teacher can get her charges absorbed and delighted by reproductions of some of the great masterpieces of the past: they love the colours, the clothes and — an actual comment — the sense of peace in a Claude landscape.) In all these respects it shows no inherent inferiority to the more conventional cognitively based curriculum. It is simply founded on different and, in some respects, more fundamental principles. Properly handled it involves potentialities of discipline and structure to exactly the same extent as the cognitive approach.

Many of these criticisms, indeed, stem from a philistine inability to assess the potential of what I am offering. It would be a thousand pities, now that it is being realized, in some degree, that the crisis is cultural — a significant advance beyond the naivety of those who for so long have seen the dilemmas of secondary education in exclusively organizational terms — if the *quality* of any alternative offering were not the prior consideration. It is, I have suggested, over the question of quality that attempts to build an alternative curriculum on the indigenous working-class culture must founder. But there is much more of what today is regarded as 'high culture' that is within the competence of ordinary children to grasp once it is made manifest in concrete form.

Clearly these suggestions are offered for debate in what has become a major twentieth-century problem — how do we cope with something new in the history of mankind, a total school population? I lack the arrogance of the comprehensivists, who would impose their schemes on everybody by law; and I shall be satisfied if in a few schools a few teachers are stimulated to look to their procedures, to question their current engagement, to test the validity of some of the suggestions I have made. The response from the theorists has been disappointing — some minor philosophical points which have usually stemmed from an imperfect reading of the words in front of them, and some predictable political hostility. But there has been little attempt to assess the scheme at any fundamental level — at the level represented by, say, D. H. Lawrence's cry: 'For the mass of people, knowledge *must* be symbolical, mythical, dynamic' (1933,

p. 68). For clearly, though there is much with which I would disagree in Lawrence's educational ideas, my analysis owes something to his influence, to his quite fundamental critique of our modern education.

Indeed, no one has spotted the great practical question mark that hangs over the whole endeavour. For, even if acceptable, what I have to offer will stand or fall ultimately by the quality of the teachers who will have to put it into operation. Here I have wavered between optimism and pessimism. I am optimistic because I believe that there is a sizeable minority of teachers who would themselves welcome a change of orientation; there are many teachers in our schools today who are having to transmit a curriculum in which they do not really believe, and which they themselves, though they may have acquired a limited technical competence in the fields in which they teach, have failed to internalize in any significant way. We should face up to the implications of the fact that their culture is as fully oriented to the popular media as to that based on literacy and the book; critical analyses of these other media might offer to them a more satisfying cultural experience, with corresponding improvement in their commitment to the educational enterprise.

But it is the *quality* of that commitment which would then be in question. As I have said elsewhere, 'My fear is that in seeking the implementation of what I am recommending I may simply be opening the floodgates to an avalanche of exploitable pop instead of the training (slow but possible) in affective discrimination I intend' (1973, p. 13). Or again, 'progressive' fears of interference with children's spontaneous likings will inhibit teachers from playing the very positive role that will be necessary in introducing pupils to material of the quality intended. For, of course, these children, above all, will have little to offer 'creatively', as it were, out of their meagre and restricted experience; they will need to be told stories, mime characters created by others, look at pictures, use myths and legends to which they have been introduced as a basis for their dramatic work, examine the craft work of others. (Here, indeed, is a place for 'imitation'.) And where are the teachers with the necessary experience, the interest and the knowledge to perform these very positive functions? The capacity for refined emotional discrimination is as rare as high cognitive ability.

To say this is simply to stress once more that we live in an imperfect world, and that there are no *solutions* to problems of the magnitude of those with which I have been dealing in this book. All one can do is to make one's depositions and honestly and squarely face the pitfalls; by exposing the latter, indeed, one may in some appreciable degree contribute to their avoidance. Certainly, the expression of the fear serves to highlight my purpose, which is education and not recreation, discipline not indulgence. What I can point to is that, although as a whole what I am suggesting has not been tried, various of the elements do, of course, already appear in the schools. Attention to 'feelings' rather than to 'things' we owe, in considerable measure, to the progressives who latterly, at least, have stressed the importance of emotional development. Admittedly their aesthetic needs modification — but they have ensured a measure of good will it is possible to build on.

IX

Finally, I refuse to accept the model of the emotional life Professor R. S. Peters has offered us, a life that involves 'something which comes over people', as if such people exist independently of their feelings, which Professor Peters seems to think constitute an interference with their 'passivity'. 'We speak', he says, 'of judgments being disturbed, warped, heightened, sharpened and clouded by emotion', positing, it would seem, an ideal of passionless rationality as the norm from which states of feeling represent an aberration (1972, p. 469).[3] Similarly it could be said that 'to be in the grip of an intense intellectual activity' is equally 'a disturbance of intellectual equanimity'. In fact we live in our thoughts and we live in our emotions equally in accordance with our response to the world around us, and notions of 'disturbance' and 'overwhelming' are metaphors indicating intensity rather than irrationality. Of course, just as we can *think* mistakenly so we can *feel* excessively; false logic is the product of one and sentimentality of the other. Just as there are forms of argument which are necessary for right thinking so there are expressive forms of emotion which nurture adequate emotional responses. It is crucial among people who manifestly feel more than they think that we do what we can to introduce them to expressive actions for forms that are disciplinary and positively releasing just as much as we teach others to grapple with the traditional forms of knowledge for understanding. The equality we sorely need is the equality of equal appropriateness, but because of such appropriateness, necessarily different.

NOTES

1. As this book goes to press, an important article by Professor Hirst (1979) indicates that if only movement educators will drop ill-considered claims and justify their discipline in terms of skill, aesthetic value, and as a form of symbolic expression, movement education would have 'a defence as formidable as any curriculum area could hope to have' (p. 108).

2. We could avoid many of these mistakes if only we could learn to allow for what I call the TI Factor (i.e. Tolerated Inefficiency Factor), a term I have coined as likely to appeal to a statistically minded generation with its implication of scientific accuracy. Of course, it is the precise inability to be accurate in any recognizable scientific sense in human affairs that has led to the need for some such conception. Before we advocate change we should not simply recognize problems, for they are ever-present in matters concerning human beings; we must decide *whether it is better to live with the problems or seek some amelioration* (rarely a *solution* for that suggests possibilities that infrequently offer themselves in situations of any complexity).

3. Though I think my comment here justified, in fairness to Professor Peters it must be said that in other contexts his ideal would seem to be one of 'passionate' rationality.

CHAPTER 6

Problems of the Elite Curriculum

I

It is becoming increasingly clear that, as with other European countries (notably Soviet Russia), provision will have to be made for able children to receive some form of special attention. 'How can comprehensive schools best provide for their brightest pupils?' asks the 'Education forum' of even the left-inclined *Observer* (6 May 1979); and the article refers to the recent pamphlet published by the Royal Society expressing its anxieties on the teaching of science to talented children. Organization is not my topic here — but there are too many straws in the wind to doubt that the problem of the able child will provide a major challenge for the 1980s. That is why attention to the 'elite' curriculum as such hardly needs justification.

II

The nature of our elite education, which has exercised so potent an influence on our thinking about the curriculum for a whole society — for it underpins current demands for a common curriculum — has, it is hoped, been clarified to some extent both explicitly and implicitly in the first chapter. Before discussing some of the problems it poses today, however, it is desirable briefly to define its fundamental nature by drawing on the historical survey already given.

It consists of two main elements, one appertaining to the study of man and the other to that of nature, with a developing interplay between the two areas on the grounds that man is himself increasingly seen as a product of nature: hence attention to the humanities, focusing especially on what is central to man, his capacity for language and his ability to record his culture, and to the sciences (natural and social), which have developed as a result of his increasingly objective view of the world and, more recently, of himself. The latter have enabled him to abstract himself from his immediate circumstances, and have substituted objectively descriptive for mythological explanations of natural phenomena. The effect of this has been to neutralize previously accepted teleological interpretation of a wide variety of phenomena, human and natural.

Initially humanistic learning — which is still a potent influence on our curriculum — was directed to fitting men for the exercise of power in government and administration. In the process of doing so it was content to draw extensively on past models, classical and Christian, on the grounds that the broad outlines of man's moral purposiveness had been settled by revelation and/or the ancients, so that the knowledge necessary for decision making was already largely encapsulated in authoritative texts. What was needed was reassertion and the assimilation of a persuasive manner in order to make traditional virtues acceptable. Gradually, however, thought came to seek a greater autonomy, assisted by the realization that the classical experience had been deficient in certain respects; it failed, for instance, to provide an adequate insight into the immediate causes of natural or social behaviour on which men's attention had become increasingly focused. Thus Machiavelli noted a tension between how men ought to behave and how they did and realized that the practicalities of conduct were important considerations in government. Attention directed to the actualities of behaviour fostered a cultural upheaval of cosmic proportions as neutrally descriptive views of the world (which would nevertheless permit a different but predictively more accurate system of control to be instituted) were substituted for teleological. The great dilemma, however, remained the problem of man, who was both of and outside the natural world, to whom, among all the living creatures, a sense of purpose alone could be attributed.

During the course of this evolution, 'knowledge' increasingly fixed its gaze on the present rather than the past, on current behaviour rather than on interpretative systems previously laid down authoritatively. The net effect was a vast extension of consciousness as what had been accepted as habitual and prescriptive was subjected to critical questioning and an increased willingness to suspend final judgement and work in terms of reconstructible hypotheses. In the outcome, human cognition gained a vast extension of its powers and of the attention paid to it in upbringing, and questions of manner, persuasiveness, had to give way before the formidable assault of 'evidence' as the final court of arbitration guiding either acceptance or rejection. In its imaginative, symbolic way something of what has happened can be inferred from a description by W. B. Yeats of two paintings, one Renaissance, one modern, to be found in the Dublin National Gallery:

> a portrait of some Venetian gentleman by Strozzi, and Mr. Sargent's painting of President Wilson. Whatever thought broods in the dark eyes of that Venetian gentleman, has drawn its life from his whole body; it feeds upon it as the flame feeds upon the candle — and should that thought be changed, his pose would change, his very cloak would rustle for his whole body thinks. President Wilson lives only in the eyes, which are steady and intent; the flesh about the mouth is dead and the hands are dead, and the clothes suggest no movement of his body, nor any movement but that of the valet, who has brushed and folded in mechanical routine. There, all was an energy flowing outward from the nature itself; here, all is the anxious study and slight deflection of external force; there man's mind and body were predominantly subjective; here all is objective, using those words not as philosophy uses them, but as we use them in conversation. [1926, pp. 359-60]

For an energy based on a dynamic interchange in which language and bodily movement through gesture and facial expressiveness as in a theatre has been substituted an increasingly mental exposition drawing on objective evidence and appropriate forms of argumentation as the characteristic communicative paradigms of the two ways of looking at the world. In the process, language, man's most fundamental mode of communication, has increasingly shed its full connotative richness and assumed a narrower denotative role, albeit with a considerable extension of technical vocabulary. Another way of describing the same process would be to point to a loss of historical richness, of evocative overtone derived from an inwardness with the verbal echoes of a historical literary culture. It is no accident that contemporaneously with the implementation of the earlier model of human interaction there developed the metaphor of the mind as a sort of inner space, a repository, a banking system where extensive deposits might be made — or that, as men learnt to arrange their observations through various principles of organization, chiefly quantitative and mathematical, such a view of the mind has been modified to see it as an instrument, a tool.

This broad categorization of the fundamental reorientation of our culture brought about by the assimilation of scientific to traditionally humanistic emphases and the resultant tensions set up between what constitute very different approaches to life should prepare us for a consideration of the very basic curricular dilemmas it has posed.

For teleological assurance has been substituted a perpetually reconstructive scepticism; for a multiplicity of perspective that characterized Renaissance inwardness with an extensive historical literature has been substituted what Blake was perceptive enough to characterise as Newton's 'single vision'. We lack the resources of an historical speech and literature, provided, for all its shortcomings, by the intensive humanist training; memorization, 'invention' in the sense of an appeal to past precedents, a concern for the 'commonplaces', *topoi,* encapsulated a traditional wisdom to be assimilated and then deployed in contemporary usage. We have accepted too readily the surface agitation of scientific and technological change, as well as that 'depreciation of historical fact' so characteristic of the scientist,[1] forgetful of the continuity of certain categories of human problems which underlies the superficial appearance of difference. We have become too concerned with 'relevance' — a fostering of purely external 'originality' without roots or depth of substance, the attempt to make children 'critical' of what they have neither the experience nor the conceptual grasp to understand, never mind assess — to appreciate that for centuries men have thought and written on these problems, that the world was not born yesterday and that encapsulated in the past there may well be an illuminating wisdom. We suffer, indeed, from the parochialism of the present — nowhere more than in the study of education itself, where former prescriptions are almost totally ignored, at least in England, so that we rush to embrace the latest fashion without the steadying influence that a respect for the past could have fostered. We are too keen to proclaim our 'autonomy', our abstraction from historical circumstance — an inheritance from the Enlightenment — ignoring the fact, appreciated by the humanist, that every word we utter comes loaded with echoes from the past; for such is surely an important consideration when it is appreciated how language structures thought.

III

Accompanying this concern for surface agitation, this anti-historical element, one notes a tendency to experiental homogenization which at least in part is stimulated by the characteristic tendency of science to treat phenomena as identical units for the purpose of categorizing them under general laws. Science is deeply committed to the quantifiable — and what can be similarly identified must be assumed to betray equivalent features.

This characteristic of science, it seems to me, has led to a crisis in our humanistic culture that is bound to have important curricular implications. On the one hand, it has fostered curricular homogenization in terms of the common curriculum. Not only is this unsuitable at the bottom end; at the top it poses the threat of mediocritization, which constitutes the permanent danger of comprehensivization. Thus, within the school certain subjects, notably the classics, have frequently disappeared despite their importance as fundamental energising forces of our culture, humane and, indeed, even scientific. Modern languages are looked on in some quarters as elitist (with pejorative implications); when taught the aim often seems to be to foster the banalities of tourist conversation rather than to introduce to the language at its finest — in the literature. New ways of organizing knowledge threaten the orderly development of fundamental modes of categorization necessitated by the attempts to introduce coherence into the chaos of nature, with consequent trivializations that have been commented on in a previous chapter. I have no doubt, for instance, but that Professor Bernstein is correct in suggesting that the conflict between what he terms 'collection' (i.e. traditionally subject-oriented) and 'integrated' (self-explanatory) codes in the classification and framing of knowledge points to something other than a small, local disturbance and is indeed, as he

suggests, symptomatic of a moral crisis in the educational system
(1971, p. 221). The 'democratization' of knowledge implicit in the
proliferation of integrated work introduces an egalitarian element
foreign to the essential nature of knowledge itself. The blunt truth is
that 'knowledge' (understood as a corpus) demands the best minds
for its assimilation and the move from humanist knowledge to a
predominantly cognitive, scientific understanding in no way alters
its elitist commitment;[2] all it has done, partly by promulgating a
false image of scientific knowledge as open and 'democratic' (which
it ceased to be a long time ago in the major scientific disciplines)
and partly through the homogenizing implications of scientific data
— among which it would like to include the human — is to raise
expectations of cultural assimilation that are doomed to disappoint-
ment. In the meantime, to put it in the homely words of an Australian
critic, Mr A. A. Phillips, our new secondary school pupils are being
allowed to spoil the education of the elite without finding a
curriculum suitable for their needs. All this constitutes the curricular
counterpart to certain movements towards cultural homogenization
within the wider society that threatens at least our view of the
humanities. Here the facts of the situation — historical and
sociological — are extremely important, which is why I propose to
analyse the situation in some depth in order to make clear what *is*
involved, and what alternative values may be at stake.

IV

I refer, on the one hand, to manifestations of avant-gardism,
especially those that are termed the 'counter-culture' — essentially
an elite movement which consciously rejects the traditional
humanistic and even scientific culture of Europe and seeks a
manifestation implying both a different content and a different
ethic. I refer also to a homogenization of cultural experience that
mingles with these elite avant-garde cultural modes elements drawn
from the rootless media culture of the masses. The two phenomena
intertwine and cross-fertilize in ways beyond the scope of this
chapter to explore. Popular culture becomes the accepted background for some who, on grounds of expertise, qualify for elite

status. As H. L. Wilensky has pointed out as a result of his empirical investigations, 'intellectuals are increasingly tempted to play to mass audiences and expose themselves to mass culture, and this has the effect of reducing their versatility of taste and opinion, their subtlety of expression and feeling' (1964a; cf. also 1964b). At the same time, it also becomes a source of inspiration for certain accepted elite artists. I have in mind the offerings of Roy Lichtenstein and Andy Warhol, whose work has been exhibited at the Tate Gallery in London, the traditional sanctuary of Reynolds, Gainsborough and Turner. Mr Warhol is the author of that classic artistic judgement, 'I feel the less something has to say, the more perfect it is' (Morphett, 1971, p. 8). Mr Lichtenstein offers us blown up strip cartoons. In music Professor Wilfred Mellers of York University subjects the Beatles' songs to serious musical consideration with flattering results. Indeed, the application of academic scholarly techniques of analysis and the tracing of influences to pop manifestations are themselves part of the phenomenon I have in mind. In recent years the English quality press has increasingly contained regular critical articles on pop. Even if we allow — which is no doubt true — that some pop is clearly better than some other, one wonders if it deserves this scholarly attention except as a sociological phenomenon. After all, people like Jerome Kern and Cole Porter were producing a comparable level of music in the thirties, but no one made these pretentious claims for them. As distraction such music may be allowed a limited appeal; as a serious contribution it is a non-starter.

Certain types of avant-gardism and the pop-rock revolution of post-1956 share in some degree a common standpoint as the end-product of the romantic revolt, a final, almost pathological, manifestation. As Professor Mellers puts it, 'The ultimate, rediscovered primitivism of a Cage or a Feldman has parallels . . . in the surrealistic trend in modern jazz. Most interestingly it is also paralleled by mid-century developments in pop music' (1969, p. 180). A. Shaw in *The Rock Revolution* tells us that, 'Rock is a collage capable of absorbing the most diverse styles and influences. There is an increasing crossover between popular song writing and serious composition' (1969, p. 5).

Professor Mellers point out that, although in expression there are considerable differences between the elite and the pop manifestations, they 'have in common a distrust of the personal, of "individual" expression'. To neither, he continues, 'does the Christian ethic, which implies guilt and conscience and the duality of harmony, seem relevant' (1969, p. 182). A Viennese critic has pointed, to the Rousseauesque source of the modern artistic cult of natural spontaneous feeling versus civilization (J. Alvard quoted in 'The plunge into the non-figurative', 1959-60). Action painting has had clear affinities with the impulse release which is a basic characteristic of the fun ethic of the pop-rock world. And the protest, violence and visceral energy of this pop-rock world stem, in admittedly grosser and cruder forms, from roots similar to those of the Dadaism and surrealism that form part of the historical development of some of the recent avant-garde elite modes. There is a similar attack on consciousness and rationality and there are similar manifestations of 'protest', violence and antagonism to conventional civilized behaviour. In this repudiation, the avant-garde and the pop-rock world join hands. Both share the post-Rousseau debasement of considering conventions, traditions, limits as fetters and barriers; both ironically participate in the convention of unconventionality.

It was Plato who, speaking of the importance of new styles of art, said: 'The new style quietly insinuates itself into manners and customs and from there it issues a greater force . . . goes on to attack laws and constitutions, displaying the utmost impudence, until it ends by overthrowing everything, both in public and in private' (*The Republic* IV, 424c). Professor Susanne Langer, more succinctly, urges that 'the vulgarisation of art is the surest symptom of ethnic decline' (1962, p. 39). A French sociologist, Alfred Willener, has collated irrationalist forms of art, popular culture and student revolt in the Paris of 1968 in his study, *The Action-Image of Society* (1970).

V

So there is the fundamental cultural dilemma which faces the educator of our able children: to what extent is he prepared to welcome this developing cultural homogeneity, this mingling of popular and elite styles, especially in view of their irrationalist origin, or to what extent is he prepared to work for the reinforcement of traditional elite manifestations of refinement, rationality and long-term rewards that it has been the accepted job of the school for able children to foster? He must choose, for the values of the traditional educational system and those of the new irrationalists come into fundamental opposition. Yet in English schools concessions to pop music are increasingly found.[3] Even the recent, no longer new, movement towards creative expression in art and writing as a purely endogenous product of child spontaneity and self-expression — desirable though it could become — makes a comment on high cultural modes by suggesting that every man is his own artist, a view also implicit in the new improvisatory techniques which draw on audience participation as an integral part of the new avant-garde music. The B.B.C. some years ago broadcast a series of programmes 'Is an elite necessary?' under the aegis of Professor Frank Kermode. The consensus of young artists interviewed is that it is not. 'Doing one's own thing' as well as the impersonality of the 'multiple' have seemingly come to stay; the authority of greatness is strictly out among a number of the young.

At the same time the cultural reorientation to which I have alluded and which, in my view, contains a threat to the traditional form and rationality of the school, holds within it a lesson we need sorely to learn; in order to understand precisely the nature of this lesson we shall need to draw further on the historical evolution of elite education during its still classical phase. In this way we shall perhaps come to understand better the reasons for our contemporary attack on those traditional civilized values implicit in our elite curriculum, and by doing so diagnose more fully what is required as corrective.

A fundamental effect of the Renaissance, as already sufficiently emphasised, was to make literacy, and the classical learning to which literacy was the gateway, an essential element in the equipment of the ruling class. Let me now briefly extend the account already given in the first chapter of this educational revolution and its effect on the character of the elite. According to Dr R. R. Bolgar the revolution comprised two phases. In the first phase the emphasis was on the classics as examples for imitation; in the second the classics formed a rallying point for spiritual discontent. Both phases have their interest but enough has already been said about the first; it is the second which is here cogent to my argument. By the end of

the Renaissance, as Dr Bolgar points out, imitation was no longer
necessary 'in the new self-confident and highly developed culture'.

Now, men turned to the ancient literatures not so much to learn a
necessary lesson as to enjoy a salutary contrast. The republican
virtues of Rome, the good life of the Athenian heyday became
myths which served as a rallying point for spiritual discontents,
providing glimpses of a culture that was now pictured as
essentially different from the pattern of contemporary Europe.
[1954, p. 3]

In other words classicism as a cultural phenomenon allowed for
those antagonistic tendencies as well as those aspirations towards
less complex and more primitive forms of existence that are endemic
in the human condition and from which the elite is not immune. It
not only allowed for them, it contained them, drawing on the
relevant parts of Horace or Virgil, and suggested alternative life-
styles which in many cases have made their contribution to the
cultural life of Europe. For instance, the purifying forces thought
under classical guidance to be implicit in the simpler rural life
became a dynamic source of inspiration from which to view, criticize
and revitalize, for classicism transmitted its values of restraint into
both the main and the alienated streams. Perhaps one of the best
examples of what has been termed the 'retirement myth' — the idea
of the simpler, more healthy, alternative way of life — is to be found
in Pope. In his study of Pope, *The Garden and the City,* Dr
Maynard Mack has brilliantly analysed the effects of Pope's rural
classicism, manifest in his house at Twickenham, in his attempts to
suffuse the crude political behaviour of Robert Walpole with poetic
insight gained from his garden retreat. As Dr Mack says,

> Garden imagery and garden situations, in poems of all genres by
> poets of all persuasions . . . had been made the vehicle for some of
> the deepest feelings of the age . . . Moreover, the relevant classical
> texts, all those passages in the Roman writers glorifying the
> retired life — its simplicity, frugality, self-reliance, and indepen-
> dence — had been so often culled, so often translated, para-
> phrased and imitated that they had become part of the mind of
> England, and indeed of Europe. [1969, p. 21]

So the retirement myth in the seventeenth and eighteenth centuries
induced at various times a Christian search for self-purification, an
impetus towards scientific research and the cult of landscape
gardening which has so enriched the English countryside. As

E.M.W. Tillyard has put it, drawing on Maran-Sofie Røstvig's monumental study *The Happy Man: Studies in the Metamorphoses of a Classical Ideal,* 'It was not mere evasion but the setting of life in another direction' (1961, p. 79). This capacity to contain certain regressive feelings — from which we all suffer — and redeploy them at best as dynamic sources of inspiration, or at least as self-respecting sources of restraint, is not the least of the contributions of classicism to European culture, and forms a significant and vitally interesting contrast to the regressiveness implicit in our contemporary cultural mode of 'protest', its repudiation of a traditional ethic, its degeneration into violence and aggression or irresponsible escape.

How does one explain this discrepancy? What has occurred to break down the forces of restraint and self-respect in a movement that shares with its predecessor a similar element of protest but that comes to manifest itself at best in sporadic acts of charity, without any sense of constructive order.

VI

By the eighteenth century the new scientific culture was gradually obtaining the upper hand. This, as I have briefly indicated earlier, was based on different principles. For my current purposes it is enough to emphasize two features of the new culture and thus extend the account already given.

In the first place its rationality is subservient to empirical observation and grows out of the models and laws derived from such observation rather than from *a priori* premises derived from authoritative texts. It is therefore, as I have stressed, subject to change because it is based ultimately on what is hypothetical and open to reconstruction. Its explanations are accordingly tentative and contingent rather than comprehensive and definitive. In this sense it is antagonistic to the positive affirmations implicit in mythico-poetic explanations and rests ultimately on scepticism with all the emotional instability that scepticism implies. Dr Bryan Wilson has summed this up:

Whereas the knowledge of the [traditional] literati was suffused with social values — a knowledge of religious texts and moral precepts — modern knowledge is increasingly of a more objective and scientific character. Thus the values which the teacher must transmit become in some sense extrinsic to the knowledge which he is assisting young people to acquire . . . the secularisation of knowledge implies the loss, or at least the reduction of specific intrinsic value-commitment. [1970, p. 55]

The second feature of the scientific-technological mode implies an attention to means rather than ends. As Jacques Ellul has put it, 'Two factors enter into the extensive field of technical operations: consciousness and judgement . . . what was previously tentative, unconscious, and spontaneous [is brought] into the realm of clear, voluntary, and reasoned concepts . . . [This constitutes] the quest of the one best means in every field' (1965, pp. 20-1). We are dominated by the assumption that our salvation lies through increased positive knowledge and its deployment. Our culture has become problem-oriented, with the implications that somewhere solutions will be found and that these solutions will spring, as Ellul suggests, out of consciousness and judgement. Hence the domination of the technical mode in our cultural life, where, as far as possible, problems are reduced to problems of efficiency rather than of values. The effect of this is to disguise the intractability of many problems, for greater efficiency can be achieved more easily than value consensus.

What has happened to the creative artist as a result of this revolution is significant. Traditionally the writer found within the cultural order some stance indicative of the values to which he adhered — it might be within the values of the court and society, or peripherally (as I have indicated) within the alternative retreat. But both were fed by the central energizing force of the traditional classical-Christian culture. With the scientific revolution, however, and its corrosive effect on traditional teleological acceptances, increasingly the writer has been forced to seek a sustaining set of values *outside* the cultural order — in a *romanticized* Nature, for instance, or within himself (his feelings), or in some ethos remote from the civilization within which he writes. Hence, there has developed among the elite avant-garde a sense of alienation and antagonism, a cult of the primitive, a degeneration into 'absurdity'; there appears to be nothing to sustain a more positive approach. At worst, the artist relapses into pure solipsism.

The expansion of knowledge that has accompanied the development of science has also had specifically educational implications; these have become manifest in the conflicting claims of general versus special education. Briefly, the problem is to find a principle in terms of which the requirements of general education can be met now that its central beliefs have been destroyed with the abandonment of the mythical cohesive power of the traditional classical-Christian culture. The modern curriculum, as has been made clear in this book, has adopted a changed principle of organization; it now exists in the neutral terms of the autonomy of mind rather than in the ethical terms of the earlier principle of organization. We have seen the emergence of a pluralistic society and the fragmented educational experiences that are becoming its characteristic features — fragmented because of the increasing need for specialization; we are increasingly submitted to the brutality of minds that know a great deal about a little but not much about anything else. We have sought to meet this situation through various integrative devices: through progressivism, which appeals to daily experience as offering a totality at odds with the supposed artificiality of subject divisions, or by adding to a specialized education what are referred to as general studies. Neither of these attempts has been successful because in neither case has any central organizing experience been discovered in terms of which either daily life or general studies can be made morally coherent. Man's life remains obstinately dominated by at least the illusion of purposiveness and the necessities of *choice*, and 'general' education must recognize this implicit obligation to meet a moral need. Commitment to the expansion of mind as such fails to meet this need. The mind is constituted of the known; it offers no priorities among the known.

VII

What, then, marks our current plurality is the scepticism on which ultimately its culture is founded. And it is because of this scepticism, I think, that perhaps we begin to see the nature and attractions of avant-gardism and the counter-culture to which I have drawn attention. The classical experience encompassed its own counter-culture. *Its* rural ideal, as I have said, allowed for those tendencies to regression endemic in the human condition, but ultimately this was regarded as a source of inspiration for the perfection of personal and social life. It represented the assertion of alternative disciplines within the same classical order. Our present counter-culture is marked by certain features that indicate its mythico-poetic function, but it is also characterized by a romantic extremism which rejects rather than seeks to ameliorate current society. It is anti-rational, stressing the virtues of spontaneity and chance; it is egalitarian in that it rejects traditional forms; it stresses the cult of experience and of heightened participation (if necessary through drugs) in typically romantic fashion; its politics are marked not by rational assessments — 'The Art of the Possible', to quote the title of Lord Butler's memoirs — but by an apocalyptic vision manifest in its appeal to remote charismatic political father-figures; it is eclectic in that it draws on many alien cultures; it is even anti-technocratic and against the society and the hierarchy implicit in technocracy. All these features constitute forms of primitivism of which the outward symbols are unkemptness, the proletarianization of student uniform, simplistic political thinking and impulse abandon, which are equally manifest in many countries. What we are witnessing, indeed, is nineteenth-century Bohemia (defined as something outside the bourgeois cultural order) up-dated, proletarianized and become in some of its manifestations viciously aggressive.

What is alarming is that this elite primitivism, as has been made clear, is counterbalanced by no reorientation to a finer order, such as constituted a potentiality of the classical retreat. All we have is the irresponsibility of an elite anti-elitism, for, in general, it has been characteristic of romanticism to repudiate forms of organization as such. Hence, for instance, the romantic has often by-passed the problem of power in public affairs, for he has been the chronicler of the private, not the public life; his interest has been in the individual, not the citizen. Power he has analysed with considerable clarity in interpersonal relationships; but power as a necessary element in the right ordering of civic life he has either ignored or scorned. Romantic political thinking has been characterized by its lack of restraint, its commitment to revolution, violence and 'liberation' with no clear realization of the need for order. In their repudiation of the abstract rationalism of the Enlightenment, the romantics failed to develop an alternative public ethic and thus to provide an alternative, steadying influence. So when the romantic enters the public realm — and he cannot finally ignore it — he is left at the mercy of his purely private dreams. Classical primitivism never lost touch with the conditions of public responsibility, the sense of a public, if simplified, order; romantic primitivism, lacking any defined sense of the public except in antagonism, has little or no insights into any necessary restraints.

VIII

We need, however, to probe the significance of these current assaults on civility more deeply to discover if there are any educational lessons to be learnt from them. In fact the counter-culture and its accompanying pop-rock culture indicate a significant lack in the Benthamite empirical calculus of the modern world. Normally these manifestations would appear characteristically as socially deviant groups that every society spawns and the parent culture should prove strong enough to contain them. But the modern establishment is fundamentally liberal in orientation and, as Eliot has pointed out, liberalism is something it is better to start from — it lacks the emotional power of a positive commitment, other than to something vaguely definable as 'progressive' in line with its permeation by an outlook fundamentally scientific and therefore 'open'. What, then, the romantic radicalization of the young implies is a search for a commitment, a myth, an ultimate meaning (even civic) in a situation where there is a felt lack of any cohesive unifying force.

No educational system can provide such a myth. Nevertheless the university and the school system can foster a commitment to the traditional culture as a totality, once the full complexities of the present cultural situation I have attempted to describe are realized. Let me spell out more fully what I mean. To do so necessitates the recognition of the importance of an historical orientation, a willingness to learn from the past. And here the humanists can help us.

Early humanist education has been much criticized — and clearly there were many features of it (brutality for instance, the dangers of a posturing insincerity or a mechanical copying of other people's style) that would be rightly unacceptable today. Yet there is a good deal of evidence that its central doctrine of 'imitation' — so foreign in many respects to our current approved concepts — worked positively in certain well-documented cases to foster the incredible artistic creativity that marked the Renaissance, a creativity that contrasts so markedly with the thinness of contemporary avant-gardism, its too easy degeneration into banality or solipsism. We know with reasonable certainty that both Shakespeare and Milton were the products of schools where the curriculum was typically humanistic, and we know from scholarly analyses of Shakespeare's plays and Milton's works that in both cases the precise nature of their poetry was influenced heavily by the classical models studied and the rhetorical training they received (cf. Baldwin, 1944; Clark, 1948). Even critics hostile to humanistic training have had to admit its potency as a preparatory influence (cf. Bolgar, 1971[4]).

The essence of the humanist doctrine involved the saturation of the pupil in the material of discourse with a view to his internalization of the best available models and his redeployment of the elegance achieved in a personal way. Characteristically they tended to speak of 'fashioning' and 'moulding' in their educational theorizing, as of pre-existent material; in general, 'creativity' with its implication, derived from its original source of the 'Creator', of making something out of nothing, belongs to the romantic movement — as does the current stress on 'originality', with its encouragement of premature, ill-gestated utterance or composition. In the Renaissance men may have made something new, but its novelty sprang out of an inwardness with traditional forms. As Professor Gombrich has pointed out, art is the product of art more than it is of nature. 'Making', as he puts it, 'comes before matching' (1962, *passim.*), by which he implies that great artists are primarily the product of the tradition rather than of the innocent eye. Picasso, of all people, complained that 'as soon as art had lost all link with tradition, and the kind of liberation that came in with Impressionism permitted every painter to do what he wanted to do, painting was finished' (quoted in Gilot and Lake, 1966, pp. 68-9).

There are, I believe, lessons to be learnt for our elite curriculum from these earlier practices. One relates to its severity. In these child-centred days we are much more likely to err on the side of flexibility than of rigidity. Whatever concessions to immediate interest may need to be made for the less academically inclined, the internal motivation and the social ambience from which he is likely to spring tend to make the able child highly tolerant of initial 'drudgery' so that a firm foundation of technique and expressive precision in whatever medium can be anticipated. Neither contemporaneity nor superficial attractiveness are necessary as spurs.

The fact of the matter is that our able children not only require a specific curriculum — but they can appreciate a more rigorous application of it. I do not believe that any children require the trivialization and indulgence that characterize the more debased forms of progressivism, but they are peculiarly unnecessary for the able, which is one good reason why bright children need to be taught on their own — apart from their more backward brethren, that is, even if, built into the more informal structure of the school (games, house organization, 'out-of-school activities'), there could be opportunities for contact.

So, to get down to fundamentals, in considering the moral implications of the modern curriculum, one founded on the instabilities, and within the amoral context, of a scientific culture, it is necessary to learn from traditional humanism, with its commitment to an essentially moral enlightenment that did not shrink from transmitting its values as necessitating, at the least, consideration. This, indeed, constituted its major attraction in an education directed to the elucidation and amelioration of the central human problems of the exercise of social and political power. No doubt the humanistic emphasis on mode and manners as well as on a specifically moral content is no longer, in a democratic age, reasonable; we are too ambivalent over matters of 'sincerity' easily to recover the necessary artificialities of a more aristocratic age, though it could at least be recognized that human beings are doomed to be artificial in the sense that their development results, in part at least, from conscious decision and does not constitute a 'natural' growth as does that of a plant or animal. One outcome encouraged by our concern for 'sincerity' or 'authenticity' has been our acceptance of regressive, more primitive models in place of more refined ones. But I have dealt with this at length elsewhere (1980).

But over the central issue of moral commitment what I am suggesting is that, in addition to our philosophic concern in education with strictly fashionable because contemporary concepts like 'autonomy', 'creativity', 'indoctrination' (the last a current 'boo-word'), we should explore the potentialities and implications of a very different set, including 'imitation', 'memory' and 'habit'. After all, in our enthusiasm for cognitive and moral freedom as our curricular purpose it is as well to recall that it was the author of *Areopagitica* who saw as the goal of his ideal school 'a special reinforcement of constant and sound *endoctrinating* to set them right and firm, instructing them more amply in the knowledge of Virtue and the hatred of Vice' (Milton in Sizer, ed., 1964, p. 58; my italics). To the further question of justification of attention to a traditional and morally enlightening literature I shall have more to say later. For the moment I will simply point to the absurdity of any successor of the great Puritan radical seeking to attribute to him, in the language of contemporary demonology, a 'fascist' intent.

We need, then, an awareness of the disruptive influence which, as an outcome of curricular change, a too rapid assimilation of its new scientific element (with its necessary orientation to the new) has had on our scholastic folk-ways; so that concepts with a limited relevance in these new fields are in danger of subverting the potential richness of areas where their application is less justified. To be more precise, literary, linguistic and historical studies require techniques of assimilation necessarily different from those apper-taining in areas experientially different; scientific study invites an ahistorical approach, implying a conceptual readiness for any necessary reconstruction. Thus, in essence, Einstein *replaces* Newton. But such substitutions play no part in humanistic matters; Eliot in no way replaces Shakespeare. Essentially we have here the distinction between an historical, literary culture and a necessarily contemporary, scientific one; and the first of our major curricular dilemmas lies in our inability to discriminate sufficiently between the two, *so that as we once allowed a historical orientation to stultify our contemporary grasp of physical actuality, so now our obsession with the contemporary robs us too frequently of what historical experience could afford, especially in its moral dimension.*

What, then, I am trying to urge is, initially, a clearer diagnostic insight into the tensions of historicity and contemporaneity that characterize the two basic elements of which our elite curriculum is made up. Science needs the contemporary — its orientation is to the future, to reconstruction (though, in the light of Professor Kuhn's arguments in *The Structure of Scientific Revolutions,* perhaps less frequently than some thinkers, such as Dewey, would have us believe). One accepts that much of the last century's science has been superseded. This is never the case with the humanities or the fine arts. In science, reconstruction means progress; change in the other fields never *necessarily* implies improvement. Unconsciously our counter-culture bears witness to this truth; it constitutes, naively, inadequately but inevitably, a search for a commitment that it fails to find in a culture riven by aspirations after the new in a way that offends against the fundamental demands of the moral nature, with its need to draw on values and principles as well as configurations of facts. Moral change may take place; but it is infinitely slower and is subjected to quite different techniques of validation from those leading to the enunciation of physical law. Hence the degradation I have briefly charted in this chapter, a degradation that stems, basically, from a failure of moral nerve on the part of educationists who fear the indictment of 'endoctrination', though indeed they might take heart from the fact that indoctrination into an historical literature, with its multiplicity of viewpoints, is a very different matter from initiation into a religious doctrinal system.

IX

This last point, indeed, is sufficiently crucial to require a little further elucidation. It is clear, for instance, that the forced initiation into classical literature that characterized the Renaissance, far from being restrictive, positively encouraged the mental freedom and boldness that characterize literary and artistic creativity of the period; for a literature, unlike a religious dogmatic system, is not monotonal in its allegiance. A literature necessarily encompasses a multiplicity of viewpoints — and this would be transmitted through any initiation into our vernacular historical literature. To clarify what I mean: it is often alleged that the *Scrutiny* list of 'approved' authors implies a great narrowness of outlook. A moment's consideration will indicate the absurdity of such a contention. If one considers three near contemporary examples alone, James, Conrad and Lawrence, one must be immediately struck at the width of perspective that would be afforded by their assimilation: their outlooks, social viewpoints, values are immensely different. All that they share is a moral concern and seriousness, not an orthodoxy.

'Endoctrination' in these terms, which are the terms intended by the humanist Milton, would be a very different matter from the 'indoctrination' feared by some of our contemporary philosophers. The only commitment is to seriousness of moral concern, a willingness to learn from formal moral commitments, and a determination to probe the significance of moral dilemmas.

But it is precisely to ensure that seriousness of moral concern that the commitment must be to a study of considerable historical depth, for the immediately contemporary has been too exposed to the trivialisation of the avant-garde (analysed above) to serve on its own. Romanticism in its decline has developed those perversities I have chronicled — it must, to ensure a genuine possibility of choice, be balanced by the sanities of a more classical age. Thus what currently appears as subversive will be challenged by an experience implying a more settled sense of order — and a richer insight into humanity's perennial problems be afforded. The cult of excessive contemporaneity implies a restrictiveness beside which my recommendation of 'endoctrination' appears liberality itself. And this goes for the arts (sculpture, painting, etc.) as well as for the traditional literary, humanistic subjects.

X

To some extent, of course, the situation I have analysed has been exacerbated by that extension of consciousness to which modern European civilisation has become committed. This, it should be made clear, has offered opportunities as well as dilemmas. And we must accept that the process of bringing under reasoned assessment what has often formerly been left to habit and tradition will continue. It is itself a process that accelerated during the Renaissance, which developed it with particular reference to what it considered the central problem of education, the problem of power. At bottom, Renaissance education was directed to conduct in this world and to the cultivation of the political virtues, republican or princely. Indeed, one of the reasons why I have so constantly used the Renaissance as one of the poles within which in this book I have carried out curricular discussion lies in the fact that it seems to me, to an extent that is certainly not true of the medieval world, to lie within a basically analogous period of secularization to that of our own times. Profound though the differences are, we recognize in the Renaissance the roots of the modern phase of European history, and this means that we should pay particular, though not, of course, slavish, attention to diagnostic clues within that period so we can detect that which may afford insights into our own discontents.

I have referred above to the neglect by the romantics of the problem of civil authority. Modern education, too, committed to the liberalizing of mind, largely ignores it though there have been recent attempts to foster an interest in political education. The fact of the matter is — and both humanists and our contemporary radicals in very different ways recognize it — that behind all curricular recommendations lies, in one guise or another, the problem of *power*. Humanists explicitly accepted this by making knowledge central to their civically oriented education; our radicals have concealed their own political intent behind a facade of indignation concerning the 'symbolic violence' perpetrated by 'bourgeois' curricular provision.

Yet the mere mention of power is calculated to send shudders down the spines of our liberal intelligentsia who when not ignoring it simply regard power as something negotiable through democratic processes. It is surely time that we faced up to the fact that all complex (and most simple) societies require the presence of elites who participate, unequally within the community as a whole, in the distribution of power and influence, and made necessary educational provision; for ultimately all societies rest on power — and in its crudest form, force. Our radicals, of course, are well aware of this disconcerting and perennial human vagary; our liberals prefer to shut their eyes to the fact.

It is for this reason that, unlike the humanist curriculum, our modern syllabuses nowhere make any explicit recognition of this unpalatable fact. Humanist education for power involved a concern for both matter and manner. 'Matter', as should by now be clear, involved the internalization of a largely political literature, affording insight into the moral virtues as activating principles, absorbing the thought categories of peoples — the Romans and the Greeks — who had given intensive attention to the business of politics. This was something very different from recent and tentative attempts to introduce 'political education' into our schools. The latter involves, in general, learning about political systems; the former afforded an insight into the complexities of practical decision making. The latter lays itself open to possibilities of biased presentation in the advocacy of specific systematic emphases; the former opens the way to a consideration of the generic problems that all political systems must face.

The *sort* of exercise I have in mind can be gleaned from this extract from Erasmus' *De Ratione Studii:*

> When the time comes to set themes for the boys' exercise, the teacher should take care lest (as happens too often) he set a theme unsuitable in subject or insipid in phrasing; let him rather set a theme that has vigor of expression or attractiveness of idea, one not too remote from the boys' own interests, so that what the boys learn in the interim will prepare them for more serious studies in the future. The themes the teacher sets the boys may be drawn from history. For example: 'The rash impetuousity of Marcellus ruined the affairs of Rome; the prudent delay of Fabius restored them.' Here is an underlying moral idea, that rash counsels too seldom lead to a happy outcome. Again, and this is a difficult one, 'Which of the two was more foolish, Orates, who threw his gold into the sea, or Midas, who thought that nothing was more precious than gold?' Again, 'Unrestrained eloquence brought destruction to Demosthenes and Cicero.' Or again, 'No praise can exceed the merits of King Codrus, who held that his own life should be expended for the safety of his subjects.' But it is no great trouble to collect plenty such themes from the historiographers, especially from Valerius Maximus.
>
> Or you may draw themes from fables, thus 'Hercules gained immortality for himself by destroying monsters.' 'The Muses rejoice in the fountain and the grove; they shun the smoky cities of men.' Or one can draw themes from apologues thus 'It is not right to burden a friend with a difficulty that you are able to take care of yourself.' [quoted in Clark, 1948, p. 214]

Clearly, none of these 'themes' would be suitable for the modern pupil; I adduce them only in order to show the *type* of subject that would be desirable, one that would avoid the dangers of specific political commitments and yet raise issues that could be relevant to the workings of any political system, issues furthermore which from the examples given are clearly subject to argument — argument, however, that would exist within the moral parameters implied by the 'endoctrination' into an historical literature that, in the terms set out above, necessarily contained classical as well as nearer contemporary romantic elements (albeit, of course, in the vernacular rather than in Latin).

Here, then, is the second dilemma I detect in our present elite education. How does one educate, not for 'politics' but for *power,* which inevitably underlies politics? While the democratic consensus persisted, one might be justified in regarding the issue as peripheral. But there are signs that the liberal democratic consensus is breaking down and the educational system must recognize the fact. My suggestion, within the compass of a small book, inevitably remains evocative rather than exhaustive; but the same principle of attention to historical models, to a realization that men have perpetually faced these problems, which cannot be solved like technical or scientific problems, and that their suggestions are worthy of consideration, applies.[5]

But then one faces the last great problem. How does one *justify* in contemporary terms, that are essentially critical and questioning and must be faced as such, *any* curriculum decision (and, especially, any discussion of discrimination within the curricular framework), never mind one somewhat unfashionably historically oriented?

NOTES

1. cf. Kuhn (1970, p. 138): 'The depreciation of historical fact is deeply, and probably functionally, ingrained in the ideology of the scientific profession.'
2. cf. Barzun (1961): 'Western society today may be said to harbour science like a foreign god, powerful and mysterious. Our lives are changed by its handiwork but the population of the West is as far from understanding the nature of this strange power as a remote peasant of the Middle Ages may have been from understanding the theology of St. Thomas Aquinas.'
3. How excellent an idea is the *Times Educational Supplement's* sponsoring of the School Proms; how saddening and frustrating to find so much energy devoted to the playing of 'pop'. Is it really worth the time, effort (and talent) needed to rehearse Glen Miller's signature tune by a secondary school when one can find a primary school offering extracts from Purcell? Yet nobody, so far as I can discover, protests. Indeed, the BBC commentator seems to rejoice in the fact that such eclecticism will 'break down snobbery'.
4. In a broadly unfavourable comment on humanist education — with which I would in some degree quarrel — Dr Bolgar suggests that 'If the schools had a role, it was a preparatory one. By guaranteeing a minimum of literacy and intellectual interest, they created an environment in which self-education could flourish' (1971, pp. 17-18). If they did that, my contention would be that they accomplished a great deal — more than many schools today, in fact.

5. In his research into children's moral judgements in history, Dr Hallam indicates that 'many subjects showed that they were ready to discuss moral problems in history from the chronological age of twelve upwards' and finds that 'many children actually enjoy such lessons'. Analogous questions to those posed by Erasmus would then seem possible with able children at least, and appeal to humanistic practice not the outrageous regressive move it will no doubt seem to some people at first sight (cf. Hallam, 1969b, pp. 200-6). Clearly, questions raising moral perplexity in power situations would need to take into account the dynamics of democratic dilemmas — a good example would be Sir Robert Mark's suggestion that today the police have to win without seeming to do so. But of course, historical or contemporary, the matter requires fuller treatment than I have time for here; nevertheless, given that any elite comes to wield power, the matter requires more airing than it normally gets.

CHAPTER 7

The Process of Justification

I

Nowhere is the current crisis in our schooling more clearly demonstrated than in the efforts that are currently made, notably by philosophers of education, to justify the recommendations that, covertly at least, they are prepared to make. I say 'covertly' because according to their contemporary remit, philosophers undertake second order activities concerned with the elucidation of concepts or the nature and adequacy of arguments; they do not aim to be prescriptive. And yet, of course, the very association of 'education' with notions of 'worthwhileness' raises questions concerning how one justifies the 'worthwhile'; what grounds are there for thinking that some activities (e.g. poetry) should appear in curricula and some (e.g. pushpin) should not? Whereas in times of comparative stability the question could go by default — the traditional is not likely to be challenged — the contents of this book so far should provide a sufficiently convincing argument that the times are not stable and that, under attack, as should by now be clear, from a variety of sources, the 'traditional' curriculum — the elite curriculum that constitutes also the basis of the 'liberally' defined common curriculum — requires justification.

A number of efforts have been made to provide it. They are usually characterized by an attempt to provide a single principle of legitimization to which appeal can be made when required. There are the transcendental arguments of Professor Peters, the appeal to utilitarian happiness on the part of Dr Barrow, the frequent evocation of the priority of autonomy by a number of educational philosophers — Mr J. P. White among others. There are two

127

features of these principles of justification that require comment: one is the surprising if comparative lack of empirical evidence evoked in support of any specific justifying consideration; the other the tendency to appeal to a single overall principle rather than to proceed, as is perfectly reasonable in ethical discussion, to call on a number of persuasive arguments evoking various principles intended to support a value judgement. I will consider each of these in turn.

In his book *Common Sense and the Curriculum* Dr Barrow takes up the utilitarian position in support of his compulsory curriculum that is to be followed by all children — a 'hard core of pursuits that it is worthwhile that children should follow' because by doing so they will promote the greatest happiness of the greatest number. The argument sustaining his particular recommendations is conducted almost entirely in terms of the desirable characteristics of the 'subjects' under review in the light of their happiness-promoting potential: sports and games will keep children healthy and happy, scientific pursuits are exhaustively analysed so as to reveal what is necessary for the 'maximisation of pleasure' (1976, p. 27), the same with mathematics and so on. What, however, is lacking — and the omission is surprising in these child-centred days — is any reference to what may be broadly termed the practicalities of the situation, and among these I would include the psychological and cultural potential of sections of the school population. Dr Barrow (and the same is true of Mr White) is prepared to make universal recommendations in the spirit of eighteenth-century uniformitarianism as if the intervening two centuries of psychological and cultural sociological analysis — providing relevant facts — had never taken place. There are very minor exceptions to this stricture: I have already referred to Mr White's brief and unjustified objections to my position, which is about as far as he goes to meet any empirical objections that might upset the beautiful abstract symmetry of his recommendations. Dr Barrow briefly admits that proposing a common curriculum does not necessarily involve proposing a common teaching approach or the assumption that all will make the same degree of progress in all the compulsory aspects (p. 105).

He has a reference to 'what it is realistic to hope to achieve' in his comments on a scientific education; he appeals to a different methodology (undefined) to support his contention that 'it is very difficult to believe that it must prove impossible to introduce the vast majority of children to this content' (p. 161). But there is no reference to any of the psychological work done on children's concept formation or, for example, to the investigations into specific aspects of teaching undertaken by Mr Michael Shayer (in science), Dr Hallam (in history) and others, which have demonstrated the too great presumptiveness of, for instance, Nuffield Chemistry. There is no mention of motivational factors that are clearly going to affect curriculum choices, no reference to the extensive work on linguistic codes, no attempts to assess the cultural stimulus of various kinds of social and historical background despite the sociological evidence available.

It is arguable, of course, that these factors are most likely to affect curricular decisions relevant to less able children. But my comments are intended to illumine a point relevant to any sort of justificatory principle evoked to support curricular recommendations. To indicate more fully what I mean, let me pass to the second of my two strictures on current justificatory exercises on the part of philosophers, the tendency to evoke a single principle — happiness, or autonomy or an intrinsic value.

It seems to me that the justification of the subjects of a curriculum operates in much the same way as any other ethical justification; in which case there must surely be times when principles conflict. It is good to tell the truth; it is good to be kind to people. Does one then *always* tell the cancer patient he is dying of cancer? Circumstances may well alter decisions: this man wants to know and can take it; this one will be totally crushed and shattered and his last weeks of life will be utterly devastated (one can never be certain, of course, for one is not God — but one makes a rational and informed decision on what one knows of the two men).

In the same way, justification of a course of curriculum action involves the weighing of both desirable principles and the facts of the case. For instance, how do I justify the emphasis I have placed on modern educational dance for the less able? I begin by describing the virtues of dance — its role as an art form, the elements of consciousness and mind necessitated in the creation of particular dances, its relation to the concreteness and actualities of conduct and hence its reliance on observation and on the appreciation of certain truths of behaviour, its evocation of an alternative 'language' to that of words, its relevance to emotional expression and hence its potential role in the education of the emotions, its associations with other arts, especially music — and so on. I then draw on psychological evidence relevant to the mentality of less able children, their fixation during the majority at least of their school life at the level of Piaget's concrete operations; I adduce empirical evidence concerning motivation and their involvement, extra-murally as it were, in dance and music, further empirical evidence concerning their actual enthusiasm for dance as a school subject — and so on. It then becomes necessary to weigh these claims against other claims for limited time allocation. In the end I have produced a number of justifications — truth-value, happiness, self-expression (and hence autonomy in one of its guises) — and found the empirical evidence supportive (other empirical evidence about the cultural deficiencies of teachers might militate against such a suggestion — but here one might take a calculated risk).

Then such a curriculum subject should also be introduced for able children? Not necessarily; the empirical evidence is now different. There would be good grounds for considering a much wider range of possibilities for able children, whose capacity for grasping abstractions would appear to be much greater and for whom, therefore, the choices are more extensive. Furthermore, the *social* responsibilities of able children are likely in the outcome to be much wider and they require a more intensive introduction to them. The values implicit in dance remain the same, but other 'subjects' with a competing range of values now jostle for preference. In the end, after careful consideration of all the evidence — philosophers are always talking about evidence: why don't they make greater use of it? — I might decide (I *would* decide) that dance should be an option (in place of sport) for able children; it would remain obligatory for the less able ones. Time only allows so much in each curriculum; values conflict. All one is asked to do is to come to conclusions that can be supported by good reasons — and some of the good reasons are supplied by empirical evidence.

One will never convince everyone — I certainly have not over dance! Clashes take place on two levels: those of values and those of fact. There will be those who will dispute that dance has the valuable features attributed to it; this is matter, in part, for demonstration. There will be those who may be willing to admit, perhaps, that dance has these valuable features but who will have none of them — they subordinate all to the politicization of the workers and these dance activities constitute bourgeois distractions. Argument is possible but may well prove abortive. It is absurd to think that one can convince all the people all the time — at the very least there are always the loonies. The point is that argument is possible and needs to be conducted in terms I have outlined.

Why the obsession with an over-riding principle? What needs to be insisted on in practical decisions of this kind is the balance of argument, argument that must have attention both to the values served and to the empirical facts supporting rejection or implementation. If my wife's former pupils really are capable of the high levels of abstraction necessary for coping with academic subjects in any extended sense, my case for dance is correspondingly weakened, I would be the first to admit. It is still an attractive and important subject but I would be willing to concede that, in relation to other possibilities, its claims are not overwhelming. For one thing, it is arguably not as *socially* useful as mastery of academic subjects tends to be. In any case, I have no quarrel with the major academic subjects and I have not the slightest wish to deprive anyone capable of benefiting from them. Certainly, I have no single over-riding principle to which I would want to appeal in support of any specific judgement I make.

Furthermore, these attempts to subsume all justification under one umbrella are largely abortive. Take the matter of happiness. Happiness, in effect, becomes an umbrella word under which are subsumed a number of principles: altruism (it must be the largest amount of happiness possible for all that wins the day — and how on earth does one measure that? Clearly, however, there are occasions when one's own happiness will have to be sacrificed for the generality); satisfaction rather than contentment (the more positive word is intended to indicate that qualitative considerations are relevant — contentment is intended to evoke Socrates' pig). The outcome is that 'happiness' in effect covers a number of values that would be the better for being revealed; and indeed Dr Barrow himself gives the game away when he urges that his 'reasons for including them [i.e. his chosen subjects] vary from item to item' (1976, p. 163) — I had thought they were always supposed to be the same, that of serving the greatest happiness of the greatest number?

One could perform much the same exercise over autonomy or any other single over-arching principle of justification. Curriculum decisions are essentially practical decisions. Here Professor Hare's distinction between 'practical agreement and theoretical irrefutability', with its emphasis on the facts of the case, is useful:

> There are theoretical difficulties, connected with the possible existence of amoralists and fanatics . . . which prevent us from speaking of a derivation of moral conclusions from factual data by means of the logic of the moral concepts. But in practice if we explore the possible answers in the light of the facts and of an understanding of the questions, we are likely to reach agreement in any careful and fair and clear discussion between people that we are likely to meet. [1976, p. 19]

In the essay from which this comes, Professor Hare is referring to the Humanities Curriculum Project; and this provides an example of just the sort of practical issue that faces prescribers of curriculum. As an educational theorist — a term I have always used to describe my professional function — I am essentially involved with prescription; in the process I am concerned to support decisions, as I have indicated above, by appeal both to values and to facts, and both may be fairly numerous. I am well aware that values cannot be derived from facts, but facts can be adduced as relevant arguments to support values. Thus I am prepared in broad terms to support the traditional cognitive curriculum for bright children — with the warnings uttered in the last chapter — on a number of grounds: intellectually it is within their scope; intrinsically it serves the pursuit of truth; it provides possibilities of satisfaction and happiness, even if delayed; it offers opportunities for social commitments in a number of ways and at the same time affords openings for limited displays of intellectual autonomy — and so on. (Why, for instance, is it so often insisted that educational aims should be either 'liberal' or 'instrumental' — why can't they be *both,* at once affording intrinsic satisfactions and yet serving useful social purposes?) This is to appeal to a number of values and to seek support from a number of implied factual statements — the children have the necessary IQ, in many cases the essential home support, there are job opportunities, the scientific and humanities subjects do have the qualities assigned to them. Of course, many of these arguments are disputable — there are and are always likely to be difficulties in the way of theoretical irrefutability. All it is possible to do is to establish the reasonableness of one's case.

II

There remains, however, one further task. For I have still to meet the argument of those who would infer that it is not possible to make cultural discriminations of the sort that I am implying by my previous criticism of certain contemporary cultural modes and my corrective stress on the importance of the historical humanistic culture. I have criticized specific modern 'composers' and artists, for instance, and urged, in general terms, the superiority of some of their predecessors. There are, even among those who are sympathetic to academic values as traditionally conceived, some who seem to find the justification of such judgements problematic.

Thus in a by no means wholly antagonistic examination of my views on culture, Dr Barrow and Mr Woods nevertheless remain unclear as to 'how one sets about selecting specific works, how one distinguishes between better and worse works of literature, and how one distinguishes between different levels of culture' (Woods and Barrow, 1975, p. 178).

I find these remarks puzzling; there is clear evidence in the chapter that the authors have read my *Education in an Industrial Society,* and I would have thought that the answer to these questions was quite explicitly contained in my lengthy analysis, in that book (pp. 153-69), of the practice of F. R. Leavis, a resumé of the Leavisian methodology which shows how, through the detailed analysis of specific works of literature (and there is the whole of the Leavisian practice in numerous volumes to support the contention) it is possible slowly but inexorably to build up a discriminatory capacity for doing precisely what the authors ask for.

To be even more specific, Mr Woods and Dr Barrow seem to find it very difficult to see why ' "Greensleeves", for example, should rank as culturally valuable, whereas modern pop songs, by and large, do not' (p. 179). Let me then try to explain how one would set about making the distinction. Let us make a few comparisons between 'Greensleeves' and one of the better twentieth-century popular songs, 'Stormy Weather'. Both refer to lost or absent loves, both therefore could be described as songs of complaint. But what a difference there is in tone and feeling. What the comparison reveals is the distinction between a refined and a self-pitying personality; and this is clearly detectable in the music. The measured dignity of the one with its slightly but not oppressive melancholy; its nostalgia controlled by the essential dignity of the dance measure enables it to achieve a degree of impersonality, a *statement* of regret rather than a wallowing in it. 'Stormy Weather' has something plagently assertive about it; it lacks the restraint of the other song. It is entirely self-regarding, whereas in 'Greensleeves' the lover still calls on 'God . . . to prosper thee'. In the one case, the expression is of a known and recognized emotion; in the other, it is of one who is striving, in the midst of his regrets, to master the emotion. The control comes out in the different measures of the two songs, one indulgently plaintive, the other dignified in its restraint.

Now, of course, these judgements are disputable; but the method is clear — it is to strive to point to what is in the two songs, to offer concrete judgements, to imply that 'this and this are what we are talking about'. This is a rational procedure. It links with the procedures already indicated in the last section. It is out of a multiplicity of such judgements, carefully supported by specific reference to texts, that one gradually establishes cultural differentiation. It is difficult to offer general principles by means of which one can identify quality, which is what people often ask for — such principles are far too abstract and generalized and make identification of the particular difficult. The only way is through specific judgements; these may imply certain principles, but ones that offer themselves not as generalized comments but as enshrined and illustrated in concrete and specific cases that afford them body and substance. *Proof* by the very nature of the case cannot be offered — it would be highly irrational to expect it because *by the very nature of the evidence* it is not susceptible of presentation.

I find it difficult to understand why it is that people who would argue vehemently — when they did not dismiss as too foolish to argue — against naive judgements made by outsiders in their own fields (what if I proclaimed the pre-eminence of Joad — or worse — in the philosophical field) yet fail to see that in literary and artistic fields the procedures of reputation-establishing differ but little from those necessary in other fields to refute the sceptic — a reliance on argument, on indicating what is there, on analysis and demonstration. Of course judgements may finally differ — but so they do regarding the standing of philosophers. It is necessary to establish these points at a time when aspects of the elite curriculum, or of any curriculum for that matter, are being neglected or dismissed on the grounds that it is not possible to establish the superiority of some artistic or literary artefacts over others. Proof — to readmit the point — is in the nature of the case impossible; but sound argument drawing on detailed analysis is not; and after all, how else would a philosopher proceed if he wished to argue the overall superiority of Wittgenstein to my Joad?

Perhaps, then, it will be appreciated that the supporter of historical quality is not helpless. He has the facts of the case to appeal to — 'facts' whether they be details of the actual content of material or social or psychological facts about the audience. He can evoke principles which, despite a certain diminution of consensus that has characterized our times, are still likely to evoke a reasonably sympathetic response once attention is drawn to them. No one can ever put the world to rights; one can, however, make one's depositions so that the debate persists and the arguments continue to have currency.

III

But finally, however briefly, one needs to give some indication why 'culture' in this qualitative sense matters: surely because 'culture' is made up of the two orders of truth — truth to physical actuality (which I shall call 'Truth'), and truth to man's potential for excellence in the moral and aesthetic spheres (to which I shall refer as 'Beauty'). It is a distinguishing feature of man that he is able not only to assess 'things as they are' (which is the Truth of science) but to conceive and in some degree realize 'things as they ought to be' (which constitutes the truth of Beauty). In the human world, assessment of what *is* often needs to face the question 'But ought it to be?' It was the gradual realization — a realization that has become even more poignant in our own times — that what *is* was gradually usurping the sense of what *ought to be* that induced Keats' protest against the predominance of mere physical reality in the name of the timeless value represented by the Grecian Urn: ' "Beauty is truth, truth beauty", — that is all/Ye know on earth, and all ye need to know.' He was not entirely right, of course, because we also need to know 'Truth'. But in the context of his and our times, his protest against the usurpation of the one by the other is needed. Without these two orders man suffers a diminution in his capacities for living. That is why culture, which encompasses both, matters. Other reasons there are, too — but these certainly.

Conclusion

Are we, then, to conclude, in answer to the challenge of the Introduction, that history is all-important? Surely the answer given here is equivocal. A new situation must be met by new attempts to face it, and what is new in our secondary education is its universality. How strange, then, that we should want to apply to it an historical solution — the attempted perpetuation, for all, of a common curriculum, a cultural offering that, whatever modifications it may have undergone during the course of time, was always intended for a limited number of children for whom alone it can be shown to be appropriate. The new denizens of the schools constitute an essentially novel problem — and necessitate a novel outcome *though one that is in touch with the historical nature of their consciousness, which has hitherto largely been ignored.*[1] But then those who have traditionally been reasonably well served should not have their diet spoilt by attempted readjustments to meet the new situation at the behest of inappropriate homogenizing elements. Whatever equalities we admit with some hope of their fulfilment — equality of opportunity, equality of *consideration* — paradoxically demand, for their implementation, differentiation of provision. It is odd, indeed, that we neglect the historical where it is appropriate and apply it where it is irrelevant; and in both cases the error arises out of a profound shift in our culture, which has released forces pressing both for homogeneity and contemporaneity within a sphere — the human — where their appropriateness needs the most careful definition. It is to a clarification of this problem that I have addressed myself in this book.

NOTE

1. 'Because the answers peasants give to natural challenges are cultural, they

137

cannot be replaced by superimposing the equally cultural responses (ours) that we "extend" to them' (Freire, 1976, p. 107). Despite the unacceptability of his 'programme', there are important insights in Freire's work from which even those who like myself find themselves in profound disagreement can draw corroborative evidence.

Bibliography

ADAMS, J. (1912) *The Evolution of Educational Theory* (London: Macmillan).
ASCHAM, R. (1967) in L. V. Ryan, ed. *The Schoolmaster* (Ithaca, N.Y.: Cornell University Press).

BALDWIN, T. W. (1944) *William Shakespere's 'Smalle Latine and Lesse Greek* 2 vols (Springfield, Ill.: University of Illinois Press).
BANTOCK, G. H. (1965) The implications of literacy. Inaugural lecture at Leicester University; republished in Bantock (1967).
BANTOCK, G. H. (1963) *Education in an Industrial Society* (London: Faber).
BANTOCK, G. H. (1965) *Freedom and Authority in Education* (London: Faber).
BANTOCK, G. H. (1967) *Education, Culture and the Emotions* (London: Faber).
BANTOCK, G. H. (1968) *Culture, Industrialisation and Education* (London: Routledge).
BANTOCK, G. H. (1973) *Education in an Industrial Society,* 2nd edn (London: Faber).
BANTOCK, G. H. (1980) *Studies in the History of Educational Theory* Vol. I: *Artifice and Nature* (London: Allen and Unwin).
BARROW, R. (1976) *Common Sense and the Curriculum* (London: Allen and Unwin).
BARROW, R. (1978) *Radical Education* (London: Martin Robertson).
BARZUN, J. (1961) Introduction to S. Toulmin, *Foresight and Understanding* (London: Hutchinson).
BERNSTEIN, B. (1971) Social class, language and socialisation. In *Class, Codes and Control* Vol. I (London: Routledge).
BOLGAR, R. R. (1954) *The Classical Heritage and its Beneficiaries* (Cambridge: Cambridge University Press).
BOLGAR, R. R. (1971) Humanist education and its contribution to the Renaissance. In *The Changing Curriculum,* History of Education Society (London: Methuen).
BOURDIEU, P. and PASSERON, J. C. (1977) Foundations of a theory of symbolic violence. In *Reproduction in Education, Society and Culture* Book I (London: Sage Publications).
BOURNE, G. (1920) *Change in the Village* (London: Duckworth).
BOWEN, J. (1975) *A History of Western Education* Vol. II (London: Methuen).
BRUCE, V. (1965) *Dance and Dance Drama in Education* (Oxford: Pergamon).
BURKE, P. (1978) *Popular Culture in Early Modern Europe* (London: Temple Smith).
Business as usual — and a course in charm (1974) *Times Educational Supplement* (28 June).

CIPOLLA, C. M. (1969) *Literacy and Development in the West* (Harmondsworth: Penguin).

CLARK, D. L. (1948) *John Milton at St Paul's School* (New York: Columbia University Press).

CLARKE, F. *et al.* (n.d.) *A Review of Educational Thought* (London: Evans).

COLERIDGE, S. T. (1933) In S. Potter, ed. *Select Poetry and Prose* (London: Nonesuch Press).

COLLINGWOOD, R. G. (1955) *Principles of Art* (London: Oxford University Press).

COMENTIUS, J. A. (1896) In M. W. Keatinge, ed. and transl. *The Great Didactic* (London: Black).

DEWEY, J. (1921) *Democracy and Education* (New York: Macmillan).

DEWEY, J. (1929) *The Quest for Certainty* (New York: Milton, Balch & Co.).

DEWEY, J. (1941) In Ratner, ed. *Education To-day* (London: Allen and Unwin).

DEWEY, J. (n.d.) *The Child and the Curriculum* (Chicago: University of Chicago, Phoenix Books).

DROPKIN, S. *et al.* (1965) *Contemporary American Education* (New York: Macmillan).

DURKHEIM, E. (1977) *The Evolution of Educational Thought* (P. Collins, transl.) (London: Routledge).

ELLUL, J. (1965) *The Technological Society* (London: Cape).

FREIRE, P. (1972) *The Pedagogy of the Oppressed* (M. B. Ramos, transl.) (Harmondsworth: Penguin).

FREIRE, P. (1976) *Education: the Practice of Freedom* (London: Writers and Readers Publishing Co-operative).

FYVEL, T. R. (1960) *Insecure Offenders* (Harmondsworth: Penguin).

GARMO, C. DE (1895) *Herbart and the Herbartians* (London, Heinemann).

GILOT, F. and LAKE, C. (1966) *Life with Picasso* (Harmondsworth: Penguin).

GOMBRICH, E. H. (1962) *Art and Illusion* (London: Phaidon).

GORDON, P. and LAWTON, D. (1978) *Curriculum Change in the Nineteenth and Twentieth Centuries* (London: Hodder and Stoughton).

HALLAM, R. (1969a) Piaget and the teaching of history. *Educational Research 12*, no. 1 (November).

HALLAM, R. (1969b) Piaget and moral judgments in history. *Educational Research II*, no. 3 (June).

HALLORAN, J. D. (1964) *The Effects of Mass Communication* (Leicester: Leicester University Press).

HARE, R. M. (1976) Value education in a pluralist society. *Proceedings of the Philosophy of Education Society of Great Britain 10*, July.

HIRST, P. (1974) *Knowledge and the Curriculum* (London: Routledge).

HIRST, P. (1979) Human movement, knowledge and education. *Journal of Philosophy of Education 13.*

HORTON, R. (1971) African traditional thought and Western science. In Young (1971a).

HUXLEY, T. H. (1902) *Science and Education* (London: Macmillan).

JACKSON, B. (1976) A question of equality. In J. E. C. MacBeath, ed. *A Question of Schooling* (London: Hodder and Stoughton).

KEDDIE, N. (1971) Classroom knowledge. In Young (1971a).

KEDDIE, N., ed. (1973) *Tinker, Tailor . . . The Myth of Cultural Deprivation* (Harmondsworth: Penguin).

KING, R. (1969) *Values and Involvement in a Grammar School* (London: Routledge).

KUHN, T. S. (1970) *The Structure of Scientific Revolutions*, 2nd edn (Chicago: University of Chicago, International Encyclopedia of Unified Science).

LABOV, W. (1973) The logic of nonstandard English. In Keddie (1973).

LANGER, S. (1953) *Feeling and Form* (London: Routledge).

LANGER, S. (1962) *Philosophical Sketches* (London: Oxford University Press).

LAWRENCE, D. H. (1933) *Fantasia of the Unconscious* (London: Martin Secker).

LAYTON, D. (1973) *Science for the People* (London: Allen and Unwin).

LOCKE, J. (1922) In J. W. Adamson, ed. *The Educational Writings of John Locke* (Cambridge: Cambridge University Press).

LOCKE, J. (1947) In Wilburn, ed. *An Essay concerning Human Understanding* (London: Everyman).

MACK, M. (1969) *The Garden and the City* (London: Oxford University Press).

MELLERS, W.H. (1969) The ultimate rediscovered primitivism. In J. Eisen *The Age of Rock* (New York: Random House).

MILL, J. and J. S. (1931) In F. A. Cavenagh, ed. *On Education* (Cambridge: Cambridge University Press).

MONTAIGNE, M. DE (1958) *Essays* (Harmondsworth: Penguin Classics) (transl. J. M. Cohen).

MORPHELT, R. (1971) *Warhol* (London: Tate Gallery).

MUIR, W. (1965) *Living with Ballads* (London: Hogarth).

MULLINS, W. R. (1968) Changes in the theory of the teaching of English 1860-1940. Unpublished M. Ed. thesis, University of Leicester.

MUSGRAVE, P.W. (1968) *Society and Education in England since 1800* (London: Methuen).

MYERS, L. H. (1935) *The Root and the Flower* (London: Cape).

NIETZSCHE, F. (1956) *The Birth of Tragedy* (New York: Doubleday Anchor Books).

ONG, W. J. (1962) *The Barbarian Within* (New York: Macmillan).

OWST, G. R. (1933) *Literature and Pulpit in Medieval England* (Cambridge: Cambridge University Press).

PESTALOZZI, H. (1910) In J. A. Green and F. Collie, eds. *The Educational Writings of Pestalozzi* (London: Arnold).

PETERS, R. S. (1972) The education of the emotions. In R. F. Dearden *et al. Education and the Development of Reason* (London: Routledge).

PLATO *The Republic.*

PLATO *The Laws.*

The plunge into the non-figurative (1959-60) *Quadrant* (Australia) Summer.

POOLE, R. L. (1932) *Medieval Thought and Learning* (London: SPCK).

POSTMAN, N. (1973) The politics of reading. In Keddie (1973).

PRING, R. (1976) *Knowledge and Schooling* (London: Open Books).

QUINTON, A. (1971) Authority and autonomy in knowledge. *Proceedings of the Philosophy of Education Society of Great Britain 5,* no. 2, July (Blackwell).

READ, H. (1958) *Education through Art* (London: Faber).

REDFERN, B. (1975) Movement and Professor Bantock's theory of popular education. University of Manchester *Gazette* no. 20, Autumn.

ROUSSEAU, J. J. (1943) *Emile* (transl. B. Foxley) (London: Everyman).

SCHOOLS COUNCIL (1968) *Young School Leavers* (London: HMSO).

SEARLE, C. (1973) *This New Season* (London: Calder and Boyars).

SELLECK, R. J. W. (1968) *The New Education* (London: Pitman).

SHAW, A. (1969) *The Rock Revolution* (New York).

SIMON, J. (1974) 'New direction' sociology and comprehensive schooling. *Forum 17*, no. 1, Autumn, pp. 8-15.

SIZER, T. R., ed. (1964) *The Age of the Academics* (New York: Columbia University Press).

SPROTT, W. J. H. (1967) Society; what it is and how does it change? In Schools Council Working Paper no. 12 *The Educational Implications of Social and Economic Change* (London: HMSO).

STEVENS, F. (1960) *The Living Tradition* (London: Hutchinson).

STONE, L. (1969) Literacy and education in England, 1640-1900. *Past and Present* no. 42.

SYKES, A. J. M. (1965) Myth and attitude change. *Human Relations 18*, no. 4

TILLYARD, E. M. W. (1961) *Some Mythical Elements in English Literature* (London: Chatto and Windus).

TRILLING, L. (1966) *Beyond Culture* (London: Secker and Warburg).

TUCKWELL, P. (1971) The theatre of the subnormal. *New Society* 14 January.

VICINUS, M. (1974) *The Industrial Muse* (London: Croom Helm).

WATSON, F. (1913) *Vives on Education* (Cambridge: Cambridge University Press).

WHITE, J. P. (1973) *Towards a Compulsory Curriculum* (London: Routledge).

WILENSKY, H. L. (1964a) in *New Society* 14 May.

WILENSKY, H. L. (1964b) Mass society and mass culture: interdependence or independence? *American Sociological Review 29*, no. 2.

WILLENER, A. (1970) *The Action-Image of Society* (London: Tavistock).

WILLEY, B. (1934) *The Seventeenth Century Background* (London: Chatto and Windus).

WILLIS, P. (1977) *Learning to Labour* (Farnborough: Saxon House).

WILSON, B. (1970) *The Youth Culture and the Universities* (London: Faber).

WIND, E. (1963) *Art and Anarchy* (London: Faber).

WOODS, R. G. and BARROW, R. (1975) *An Introduction to Philosophy of Education* (London: Methuen).

WOODWARD, W. H. (1964) *Desiderius Erasmus concerning the Aim and Method of Education* (New York: Columbia University Press).

YEATS, W. B. (1926) *Autobiographies* (London: Macmillan).

YOUNG, M. F. D., ed. (1971a) *Knowledge and Control* (London: Collier-Macmillan).

YOUNG, M. F. D. (1971b) Curricula as socially organised knowledge. In Young (1971a).

Index

143

144   *Index*

politicization of, 34, 42, 50-1, 52,
   58, 63-7 *passim,* 71-7 *passim*
psychological aspects of, 16-18
   passim, 20-2 *passim,* 26-7,
   38-46 *passim,* 56, 60, 61,
   83-90 *passim,* 93-4, 99,
   104-5, 117, 119, 128, 129,
   130
science and the, 11-15, 19-21, 23-5
   passim, 28-9, 36n, 37, 40-1,
   104, 106-8 *passim,* 113-115
   passim, 119-20, 121, 125n,
   128-29
self-expression and the, 6-7, 118
subjects in the, 44-5, 107, 127-29
as 'symbolic violence', 69, 74-5,
   123
and tradition, 39-45 *passim,* 47,
   50, 52, 54-7 *passim,* 63-7
   passim, 71, 104-5, 107, 108,
   110-12 *passim,* 117-22
   passim

Dadaism, 110
Descartes, Rene, 5, 11, 14
Dewey, J., 39, 41, 42, 48, 50-58
   passim, 68, 72-73, 120
Dropkin, S., 25
Durkheim, E., 2, 7

Edinburgh Review (The), 23
education, child-centred, 17-19
   passim, 39-45 *passim,* 118-19
elite, 12, 30-1, 32-4 *passim,* Ch. 6
emotional, 88-94 *passim,* 98, 101,
   108
liberal, 23-4, 25-7 *passim,* 30,
   32-5 *passim,* 37-8, 42-3, 51,
   52, 56, 98
medieval, 3-5, 7
and morality, 3, 11, 18, 22, 30-1,
   119-22 *passim,* 132
progressive, 17, 31-4 *passim,*
   Ch. 2, 85, 90, 100-01, 115,
   118-19
and values, 16, 37-41 *passim* 43,
   45-7, 52-9 *passim,* 64-71
   passim, 92-4 *passim,* 98-9,

100, 102n, 109-11, 114,
   125n, 127-36 *passim*
vocational, 26, 37, 94, 98
Eggleston, J., 92
Einstein, A., 120
Eliot, T. S., 29, 35, 117, 120
Ellul, J., 114
empiricism, 30-1, 38
   see also experience
enlightenment, 25, 30-1, 48, 50, 107,
   116
equality, 41, 47-8, 49-54 *passim,*
   60-1, 62, 72-6 *passim,* 96-7,
   101-2, 108, 111, 128, 137
Erasmus, Desiderius, 6-9 *passim,*
   14, 124, 126n
experience, 8-10 *passim,* 12-14
   passim, 18, 19, 40-7, 67, 68, 69,
   70, 87, 98
   see also empiricism

Freire, P., 17-18, 63, 71-7, 78n, 85,
   137-38n
Freud, S., 33, 86, 94
Froebel, F., 17, 29
Fyvel, T. R., 90

Garmo, C. de, 22
Gilot, F., 118
Glazer, N., 51
Gombrich, E. H., 118
Gordon, P., 24, 27-9 *passim*

Hallam, R., 86, 126n, 129
Holloran, J. D., 93
Halsey, A. H., 51
Hare, R. M., 131-2
Hartley, David, 16-17
Harvard Report: *Liberal Education
   in a Free Society,* 26
Hemans, Mrs. F. D., 80
Herbart, J. F., 21-3 *passim,* 43, 57
Hirst, P., 25-7 *passim,* 102n
Hoggart, R., 93
Horace, 112
Horton, R., 64
humanism, 6-9, 117-18, 120, 123,
   124, 125n